THE SCIENCE OF HOCKEY

THE SCIENCE OF HOCKEY

Revised Edition

HORST WEIN

translated from the German by
DAVID BELCHAMBER, M.A.

PELHAM BOOKS
LONDON

First published in Great Britain by
PELHAM BOOKS LTD
44 Bedford Square
London WC1B 3DP
MARCH 1973
SECOND ENGLISH EDITION MAY 1979
REVISED EDITION 1985

First published in West Germany as
Hockey: Lernen und Lehren
by Verlag Karl Hofmann,
Schorndorf bei Stuttgart.
© 1985 by Horst Wein

Wein, Horst
    The science of hockey.— 2nd rev. ed.
    1. Field hockey
    I. Title
    796.35'5   GV1017.H7
    ISBN 0-7207-1531-8

All rights reserved. No part of this publication
may be recorded, stored in a retrieval system,
or transmitted, in any form or by any means,
electronic, mechanical, photocopying, recording or
otherwise, without the prior permission of the
Copyright owner

Set by Allset Composition, London.
Printed in Great Britain by
Hollen Street Press Ltd at Slough
and bound by Hunter & Foulis, Edinburgh

CONTENTS

	Preface	ix
	Technical skills in Hockey	xi
	Key to symbols	xiv
1	**The Methodical Coaching of Technical Skills**	1
2	**Dribbling — Techniques and Tactics**	5
	Dribbling on the front stick	5
	The Indian style of dribbling	9
	Looking up from the ball while dribbling	12
	Tactics in dribbling	15
3	**The Push Stroke**	17
4	**Stopping and Receiving**	23
	Stopping on the forehand	24
	The reverse-stick stop	29
	Tactical considerations before or whilst receiving the ball	35
	Stopping at penalty corner	37
5	**The Hit**	40
	The 'chipped' hit	52
	The force of the hit	52
	The shot at goal	55
	The penalty corner	57
	Disguising the direction of the hit	61
6	**The Flick**	65
	Teaching the flick	66
	Use in the game	69
7	**Beating an Opponent**	72

8 The Dummy — an essential part of modern Techniques and Tactics	88
Feinting without the ball	88
Feinting with the ball and/or the stick	90
9 Tactical Exercises to Improve the combined Attack	94
10 Running into the open space	105
Giving the pass and immediate movement into open space	111
Methodical development of the triangular pass	114
11 The Tactics of Passing	120
Accuracy in direction	121
The timing of the pass	122
The speed (force) of the pass	123
Disguising the direction of the pass	123
12 The Defence — how to improve it individually and collectively	125
Factors which determine the method of tackling	126
General rules for tackling successfully	126
Positional play	127
Lunging to tackle	128
Tackling in retreat	130
Block tackle	134
Worrying the opponent when taking the ball	134
Close marking an opponent	136
Extending the defender's reach	140
Covering in defence	143
13 The last line of Defence — The theory of coaching Goalkeepers	146
Physical and psychological considerations	146
Special exercises for the goalkeeper	148
The technique and tactics of goalkeeping	152
The goalkeeper's position at the alert	152
Positional play	153
Defensive technique when making a stop	155

	Kicking	161
	The 'save-clear'	164
	The goalkeeper's role in the circle	165
	Defending a penalty stroke	168
	The goalkeeper's dress	169
14	**The Development of Team Formations**	171
	The first traces of a team formation	171
	The 'pyramid'	171
	The concept from 1962 onwards	172
	The 4 : 2 : 3 : 1 system	175
	No system endures	179
15	**What is 'Modern' Hockey?**	181
16	**The Player's Style of Running**	184
17	**Developing flexibility and dexterity**	186
18	**Some very short notes about the Psychological Preparations**	191

PREFACE

There is no clear-cut division between competition and training. Between the two exists a constant interaction. During the game, we discover what has to be practised in training and, in training, we learn new ideas which need to be tried out in a match.

This relationship between training and competition, used in conjuction with the latest knowledge derived from a scientific approach to the sport, should determine the development of any game. It has done so in the majority of Olympic sports but hardly so in hockey. This sport, since the introduction of artificial grass pitches in 1975, has developed rapidly but the evidence of the last decade suggests this knowledge has passed largely unrecorded in most parts of the world.

As a player and a coach, I have been able to gain some insight into the development of the game of hockey and, in this book, have tried to put forward my thoughts for a modern style of hockey, thoughts which I hope will act as a stimulus for further discussion.

I hope to be able to present the player with the technical and tactical foundation which will form the basis for raising his individual performance to new heights. At the same time, I have tried to give the teacher and coach ideas for drawing up coaching programmes on methodical lines, both for schools and clubs.

If, in addition, this manual, as well as my later publications of *'The Advanced Science of Hockey'* and the audio-visual F.I.H. coaching book *'See and Learn Hockey'*, helps all hockey enthusiasts to see more clearly the stages in the development of their own game and encourages them to engage in discussion, then I have attained my objective.

HORST WEIN
National Institute for Physical Education
University of Barcelona
1984

Technical skills in Hockey

Hit:

1. Hit on the left foot (pp. 40-57, 157-161).
2. Hit on the right foot (pp. 46-47, 157-161).
3. Hit with low grip (i.e. hit out p.c.) (pp. 42-43).
4. Chop (p. 45).
5. 'Chip' (p 52).
6. Disguising the direction of the hit – slice (pp. 61-64).
7. Disguising the direction of the hit – top spin (pp. 61-64).
8. Forehand slap-shot (as rebound) (*p. 159).
9. Reverse stick slap shot*.
10. Reverse stick hit (p. 47 and Fig. 51c).
11. 'Bowling' hit (in a frontal position with the right hand in centre of the stick) (pp. 19, 41-42).

Push:

1. Push in a side position (with the left or right foot brought forward) (pp. 17-22).
2. Reverse stick push (pp. 34, 96-104).
3. Disguising the direction of the push to the left (Fig. 13, pp. 96-104, 106-111).
4. Disguising the direction of the push to the right (pp. 96-104, 106-111).
5. Push-out (for penalty corner) (p. 58).
6. Push in a frontal position (as direct or wall pass) (pp. 19-22, 114-118).
7. Pushing forward from a running position (pp. 96-104, 159-161).

Flick:

1. Flick on the left foot (pp. 65-71).
2. Flick on the right foot (pp. 67-68).
3. Reverse stick flick (pp. 69-70).
4. Disguising the direction of the flick to the left (p. 67).
5. Disguising the direction of the flick to the right (p. 67).
6. Scoop (when during dribbling the ball is in front of the body or beside the left foot).

Receiving:

1. Frontal forehand stop (vertical stick position) (p. 24).
2. Frontal forehand stop (vertical stick position) with the left hand behind the handle and right hand behind the curve (for penalty corner on natural grass) (pp. 37-39).
3. Frontal forehand stop (horizontal stick position) (pp. 25-26).
4. Frontal reverse stick stop (horizontal stick position) with the left hand only or both hands on the stick (Fig. 109b, pp. 25-26).
5. Frontal reverse stick stop (horizontal stick position) with the left hand behind the curve and the right hand at the handle (for penalty corners) (pp. 37-39).
6. Side position forehand stop (diagonal stick position and horizontal stick position) (pp. 28, 36-37, 96-104, 106-111).
7. Side position reverse stick stop (diagonal stick position and horizontal stick position) with anti-clockwise turn of the stick (pp. 30-34, 36-37, 96-104, 106-111).
8. Side position reverse stick stop (diagonal or horizontal stick position) with clockwise turn of the stick (pp. 29-34).
9. Receive passes from behind on the front or reverse stick with the back pointing to the passer (pp. 28-29).

Dribbling on the Open Face:

1. Controlling the ball on the open face (without gaining much space)*.
2. Dribbling on the open face (ball always or sometimes in contact with the curve) (pp. 5-9, 12-15).
3. Dribbling on the open face with change of directions (left and right hand turn) (p. 18).
4. Dribbling on the open face with the left hand only on top of the stick*.
5. Dribbling on the open face with the right hand only on top of the stick (p. 5).

Beating an Opponent:

1. Dribbling alternatively with forehand and reverse stick in front of the body (pp. 9-12).
2. Beating an opponent on his open face side (pp. 83-87).
3. Beating an opponent on his reverse stick side (pp. 80-83).
4. Beating an opponent on his open face side with previous stick and body dummy to the opposing side (pp. 83-87).
5. Beating an opponent on his reverse stick side with previous stick and body dummy to the opposite side (pp. 83-87).

6. Beating an opponent by pushing the ball past him (with forehand or reverse stick) or above his out-stretched stick (pp. 69, 72-75).
7. Beating a man by a sudden change of direction and speed (pp. 75-80).

Deflections:

1. Forehand deflection from a pass coming from behind or from the left (as a direct pass or as shot)*.
2. Forehand deflection from a pass coming from the right (as a direct pass or as shot towards goal) (pp. 163-164).
3. Reverse stick deflection from a pass coming from the right (as shot at goal)*.

Tackles:

1. Forehand lunge (without and with stick and body dummy) (pp. 120-130).
2. Reverse stick tackle (without and with stick and body dummy when the left or right foot is in front) (p. 130).
3. Tackling in retreat with forehand (pp. 130-134).
4. Tackling in retreat with the reverse stick (pp. 130-134).
5. Jab* (pp. 134-136).
6. Block tackle (with forehand or reverse horizontally on the ground with one or two hands) (p. 134).
7. Tackle with a sudden change of the stick from one hand into the other (especially in the 1 : 2 situation) (p. 130).

Goal keeping:

1. Stopping the ball with both legs (pp. 155-157).
2. Stopping with one leg (pp. 155-157).
3. Stopping with the hand (p. 157).
4. Stopping with the stick (p. 157-158).
5. Clearing the ball with inside step kick (p. 163).
6. Clearing the ball with the toes (pp. 162).
7. Clearing the ball with the stick (with the right hand only or with both hands on the stick) (pp. 157-158).
8. Sliding – tackling (Fig. 123).
9. Running out and blocking horizontally (pp. 165-167).
10. Save – clear (pp. 164-165).

*see '*The Advanced Science of Hockey*'

KEY TO SYMBOLS

──────►	Path of the ball.
∿∿∿►	Path of the player with the ball.
─ ─ ─ ─►	Path of the player without the ball.
+	Symbol for the ball at the beginning of a practice.
▲	Defender or other member of the same team.
△	Attacker or other member of the same team.
₧	Flag or cone.

1 The Methodical Coaching of Technical Skills

In all sports, technique is built-up by passing through various graduated stages during coaching and the basic principle of working from the 'simple to the complicated' determines the sequence of these stages.

One must distinguish clearly between the following eight steps when dealing with the right, methodical teaching of techniques; of course, in reality these overlap and are only separated here for better understanding.

1. Learning the skill by standardised, but varied, types of practice.
2. Developing the skill with game-related skills.
3. Improving the skill by drills with an imaginary opponent.
4. Consolidating the skill by drills with passive opposition.
5. Perfecting the skill by drills with active opposition.
6. Putting the skill to the test in small specific games.
7. Putting the skill to the test in practice games.
8. Putting the skill to the test in a match.

Each of these stages has its own characteristics and its own special degree of difficulty. At what particular stage the coaching can be taken up, or how much time has to be spent on the individual stages depends on the previous level of achievement and progress of the individual players.

Stage 1 : Learning the skill by standardised, but varied, types of practice.

A fruitful start to practising a new skill is for the player to recognise that his game lacks something. Only when the player realises from his own experience, derived either from training sessions or his most recent match, that there is something lacking in his game, does the real significance of the practice drive home. His training is then motivated and related to the actual game.

To obtain an elementary idea of the new skill being learned, the player must first of all see it demonstrated. The particular skill must be demonstrated not just once, but several times and as the player must see very clearly how the skill is carried out, the coach must go through the exercise slowly. If he demonstrates it too quickly, it will be too difficult for the pupils to grasp entirely. So that all the players can follow easily the skill being demonstrated, it must be demonstrated from different angles, from the side as well as from the front and rear. It is vital, especially for players under the age of twelve, to see the skill repeated several times. This is much more effective than mere explanation, as young players are capable of taking in only a limited amount of abstract instruction.

An explanation, which must be as short and as comprehensible as possible, can be given before the third or fourth demonstration, in order to draw the attention of the young pupils to certain difficulties or sources of error. Demonstration and explanation should not take place simultaneously, but rather follow on from one another fairly quickly; it will be found that separating visual demonstration from verbal explanation increases receptiveness in pupils.

Practice then follows demonstration and explanation. It is usual to find that at first the pupils are unable to perform the skill without certain errors creeping in. The reasons for this are, among others, trying to perform the skill too quickly or trying to take in too many aspects of it. With frequent correction of the faults, the performance of the skill must gradually improve.

Stages 2, 3, and 4 : Develop the skill with game-related drills and improve the skill by practice with an imaginary opponent and consolidate the skill by practice with passive opposition.

With these next stages, the practice is brought more closely into line with the actual game helping the player to advance progressively from doing to using the drill. First, the new skill is linked to other skills (integrated skills coaching), then by the introduction of an imaginary opponent (e.g. cones) and then by the introduction of an opponent who remains passive for the time being. Whereas, during the first stage, the player's primary concern was to establish control over his own body, as well as over the stick and the ball, he, in addition, now has to learn to take into consideration, in the first case, the position of the opponent and the distance between the opponent and himself, (for practice with an imaginary opponent see pages 73 *et seq*, 96 *et seq*, 114 *et seq*), and, further, in the second case, to consider the way his opponent is standing as well as the distance between them in terms of both time and space (for practice with passive opposition see e.g. 73 *et seq*).

Stage 5 : Perfecting the skill by practice with active opposition.

This step represents an important transitional stage towards the game itself, as the pupils now learn to perform the skill correctly in a situation comparable to match play. As the opponent's active intervention will suddenly confront the pupils with unforeseen situations, many players experience difficulties here. If, however, during the preceding stages, the many practices have been performed in a varied manner, and the active intervention of the opponent is introduced gradually, then confidence in performing the skill quickly increases.

Experience has shown that, at this stage, situation-linked practice (i.e. that which depends on the opponent's actions) is successful only if the pupil already knows several ways of solving the problems presented and can also command the necessary technical and tactical means to perform them. In contrast to previous stages, therefore, there is now no definite laying-down of procedure. The choice of the necessary technique and tactics is left to the pupil. This depends on the degree to which he has been trained to react to his opponent's behaviour (e.g. from the latter's grip on the stick and stance) and on his correct analysis of the situation at that moment (e.g. the distance between them, his opponent's strengths and weaknesses, the disposition of his team-mates, etc.). During this important stage the player may be also obliged to perform the skill quickly (play against the stop watch) and also when tired, in order to prepare him fully for the demands of the game.

Stages 6-8 : Putting the skill to the test in small specific games and practice games and, finally in a match.

The skill which has been learnt is not an end in itself; it has been taken out, and must now be put back, into the context of the game and the value of the practice becomes clear for all to see when the skill is used successfully in a real game.

The game (small game with reduced space and number of players, practice game and the match) is therefore taken here, as one of the stages in the whole methodical process of training.

But graduations are to be seen within the framework of all kinds of games themselves. The small games in which the specific skill should be dominant can be carried out under easier conditions or more difficult ones, with modified rules and specific tasks, on smaller or full size pitches at will. On the other hand, in a practice game, all the details and outward appearances will be those of a match: e.g. full teams, the game lasting for seventy minutes, with a five to ten minute break, a proper line-up, regard for team formations and use being made of the various tactical measures in defence and attack; all these serve to prepare for the approaching match.

Small games and practice games can, and must, follow on naturally from the earlier stages in training, but must not, in any way, displace or limit systematic practice too much.

Finally, at the end of all these stages in training, comes the match.

To prepare systematically for the match, the eight stages already described must be worked through in training. A return to a previous stage is always worthwhile if the coach sees elementary faults appearing in the performance of any skill. Before training can progress these faults must first be isolated and then eradicated under easier conditions. However if a player's technique is to be extended by the introduction of new skills or is to be raised to a higher level by means of new integrated skill sequences, then all these stages must again be worked through separately.

2 Dribbling - Techniques and Tactics

Dribbling on the front stick

If an attacker, bearing down at goal, is out on his own, he can most quickly attain the game's ultimate objective — a goal or at least a clear shot at goal — by dribbling, always keeping the ball with forehand diagonally in front of his body on the right hand side. The face of the stick should be in contact with the ball at least two feet diagonally off to the right, in front of the right foot. If the ball is kept closer to the body, there is the danger of the player treading on the ball. Moreover his field of vision is reduced and he is no longer able to keep an eye on the overall situation. When dribbling on the front stick, the left hand is brought from above onto the handle at the top, so that the back of the hand does not point in the direction of the dribble but obliquely upwards to the right (*Fig. 6* and *Fig. 1a*). The right hand comes in from the right and grips the stick in the middle, so that the back of the hand points backwards. The more experienced the player the more he is able to move the right hand further up without losing precision in his dribbling (see *Fig. 59c*). Fig. 1a shows very clearly the left forearm forming an extension of the stick in a straight line.

Fig. 1a. Volker Fried (West Germany) moves the ball forward on the front stick ready to pass it in the next moment with the reverse stick under the stick of the Malaysian defender to his team-mate to the right. Observe the correct position of the left hand and the loose grip of the right hand.

If the left hand is brought in from the left onto the stick, instead of from above, no real advantage is derived at first from dribbling to the right. But in order to be prepared to play the ball on the reverse stick side and to stop the ball in any situation, players are recommended always to allow the left hand to grip from above when dribbling (see 'The Indian style of dribbling', page 9).

When tackled by an opponent from the left (right) side, it is advisable to dribble the ball only with the right (left) hand at the top of the stick in order to place the ball further to the right (left) of the body out of reach for the defender (*Fig. 1b*), a technique often demonstrated by the right wing (left wing).

The following mistakes are commonly to be found in dribbling
1. The back of the left hand does not point upwards, so that the thumb can clearly be seen by the dribbler.
2. The left wrist is bent, so that stick and left forearm no longer form a straight line, which could result in poor ball control.
3. During the dribble the stick is not held at an angle of approximately 45° to the ground.

Fig. 1b. T. van t'Hek demonstrates how to avoid a successful tackle by the Pakistani defender Mansoor sen., by keeping the ball out of the opponent's reach. Observe the running free of Leefers in the background.

4. The player keeps the ball too close to the feet, which may lead to kicking, over-running and poor vision.
5. The player's eyes are riveted to the ball (see 'Looking up from the ball while dribbling' page 12).
6. When touching the ball the stick head is advanced in relation to the position of the wrists (see photo 40 in *The Advanced Science of Hockey*')

Methodical series of practices for learning dribbling on the right.

1. Dribbling along a straight line
Each player is given a ball, which he propels forwards with a series of little taps, imparted principally by the right hand or he keeps it, especially on flat surfaces, always in contact with the curve. The coach corrects any mistakes in the grip (especially of the left hand), body position, ball position and foot-work.

2. Dribbling along a straight line with three.
a) Two players, A and B stand behind each other. A third player, C, places himself opposite A and B, 22.90m away facing the others. The first player A is given a ball, which he dribbles on the right to player C standing opposite and hands it over to him (*Fig. 2*). Now it is C's turn. After a few runs, attention should be paid to see that the players practise looking up from the ball frequently while dribbling.

FIG. 2

b) Dribbling Relay: as in a). So that players do not push the ball too far forward while dribbling, the coach must issue firm instructions, i.e. the ball must be tapped at least twelve times on the way or must be kept always in contact with the stick.

3. Dribbling round to the left:
Groups of three players line up. A cone is placed some ten metres away from each group. After players have made a few trial attempts to dribble round the cone to the left as skilfully and quickly as possible, the coach gives a demonstration. This is rounded off by a short explanation of the skill: the ball is controlled at first on the right hand side of the body; then, just before coming to the cone, it is placed directly in front of the body and finally, having dribbled round the cone, turning to the left, the ball is once more controlled on the right hand side, almost in front of the body.
  To intensify the practice, two balls can be used by each group. As soon as

the player brings the ball back onto his right hand side after running round the flag, the next player starts.

A skill necessary to beat an opponent is that of mastering to move the ball from the right side of the body, round to directly in front of the body, whilst running or sidestepping to place the body behind the moving ball.

4. *Dribbling round to the right:*
a) Again the ball is controlled on the right hand side of the body. About two metres before reaching the cone the player starts to overtake the ball keeping it level with his heel at first, then, as he begins to turn to his right, he overtakes it completely. In the course of the turn round the post, the ball, in the inner lane (inside the player), travels more slowly than the player in the outer lane. The player's right shoulder points backwards and is dropped a little as he enters the turn; at the same time the left elbow points well to the front, so that the stick face can be brought into position as quickly as possible after the turn. This movement is often used by the left wing when beating an opponent.

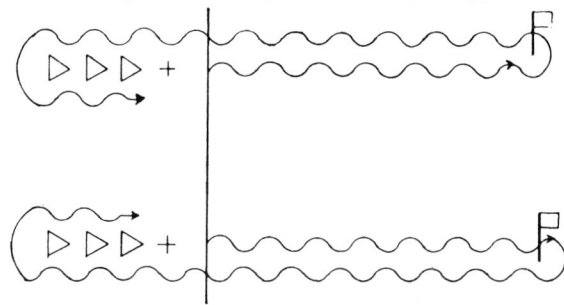

FIG. 3

b) Relay race alternately dribbling round to the left and to the right. The groups of players line up next to each other, a comfortable distance behind a marked out line. A cone is placed ten metres in front of each group. When the whistle is blown, the first player of each group dribbles to the cone, goes round the whole of his own group before passing the ball onto the next player (*Fig. 3*). Any attempt at cheating by the players will be prevented by their having to dribble round their own group. Odd numbered players must go round the cone and their own team by dribbling to the left and even numbered players by dribbling round them to the right. The relay race is over when each player has had two turns, dribbling once to the left and once to the right.

FIG. 4

5. *Slalom:*
a) Two cones are placed some six metres from each other. After a straight run of about ten metres, the player changes direction to the left, follows it with a right hand turn round the cone, and changes direction to the right again, so that the ball describes the figure 8 (*Fig. 4*). The coach must pay special attention to the position of the ball in relation to the body. When the first player reaches the first cone, the second player should start immediately, so that there is traffic in both directions.
b) Dribbling around several cones placed one behind another in a straight or very curved line varying the distances between the cones.
c) Parallel-Slalom race

6. *Dribbling races*
Around the circle, a square (*Fig. 5*) or around a triangle with and without handicap in both directions, with preference to the anti-clockwise direction in which the player is forced to dribble the ball in front of the body. Whilst in one competition the ball should be tapped on the way, in another competition the ball should remain always in contact with the stick.

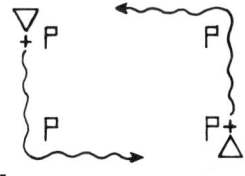
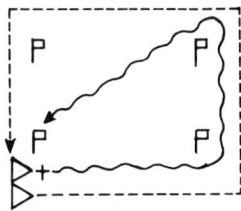

FIG. 5

The tendency in modern hockey is to favour the quick accurate pass and pickup at the expense of the dribble. But there is not always an unmarked player on one's own side to pass the ball to. In such a case, the ball must be kept under control and in certain circumstances an opponent must be outplayed to draw the defence away from a team-mate or to produce a shot at goal.

The Indian style of dribbling
Experience has shown that interest in hockey can rapidly diminish after the first few hours of practice — especially among girls — if the hit, which frequently fails to succeed, is taught at the beginning. A taste of success for the young player, his awareness of being able to master something, is guaranteed if Indian dribbling is placed at the top of the practice programme. However, if the beginner first learns the complicated hit, as is all too common, its free use in the early practice games makes the danger of injury for all participants very real; the more so since the players still lack an understanding of the

games' perspective, all congregating around the ball with the result that they are unable to avoid obstructing each other.

Controlling the ball in the orthodox manner on the right hand side of the body was the favourite method of dribbling in Germany until about 1954. It was then that members of the German national team during a four week tour of Pakistan were able to study the playing methods and stick techniques of the Pakistanis. They were stimulated to learn about Asian techniques and to adopt the Indian style of dribbling.

During their tour of Pakistan, the German players had come to recognise the advantage to be gained by controlling the ball in front of the body instead of on the right hand side. With the ball in this position they were able to produce lightning-quick passes either to the right or left or they could feint a pass to the left and, in fact, pass to the right or *vice versa*.

The Indian style of dribbling first produced certain technical difficulties which were only resolved by adopting the Indian stick with its shorter blade. Nowadays, however, learning to control the ball in front of the body has become a crucial point in any player's coaching because it prepares the ground for learning how to beat an opponent and how to sell a dummy. In Germany, indoor hockey especially encouraged the development and improvement of this style of dribbling, which today on artificial turf must be mastered by every beginner.

Because the ball is played alternately with forehand and the reverse stick, the left hand whilst dribbling must be brought in from above onto the stick and, on no account, from the left. *Fig. 6* shows quite clearly how the left hand has come in from above, and not from the left, to grip the stick. The player in the foreground on *Fig. 6* is dribbling the ball on the front stick moving diagonally forwards towards his left. The player behind him has just completed his reverse stick play, moving the ball forwards to his right; then, after turning the stick over completely (see the player in the foreground), he will again play the ball forward towards his left, dribbling the ball in the normal position.

Some preliminary exercises are necessary when coaching beginners in the Indian style of dribbling.

A simple way of showing how to grip the stick whilst dribbling and stopping is to place it flat face downwards on the ground. The beginner picks it up with both hands at the same time, the left hand nearest the end of the handle and the right hand at the lower part of the towelling. Using this grip the back of the left hand is in full view but the thumb can hardly be seen. Next each player is given a ball which he places centrally in front of his body. The stick, the face of which is touching the right of the ball, should be at an angle of 45°. From this position the player must turn the stick over, using

Fig. 6. Two German players, Engels and Thelen, practise the Indian style of dribbling

Fig. 7. The author demonstrates the Indian style

only the left arm at full stretch, so that, after a semicircular movement of the stick above the ball, the toe of the stickhead is now directly to the left of the ball, pointing downwards to the ground. The back of the left hand must be pointing downwards at this moment (see the player on the right in *Fig. 7*). A second attempt when the left hand is brought onto the stick from the left hand side will quickly convince the beginner that the correct way is to grip the stick from above with the left hand in the initial position (see the player on the left in *Fig. 7*). In fact, the further the left hand slips upwards to the right into the required position, the easier it is to play the ball on the reverse stick.

When the beginner has mastered this preliminary exercise, he again takes up his position with the feet a shoulder's width apart, now placing the ball approximately 50cm in front of his right foot. Then the left and right hands take hold of the stick in the manner already described. When turning the stick, the grip with the left hand should be firm, whilst the right hand must be kept very slack (*Fig. 1a*), so that the stick, being firmly under the control of the left hand, can be freely turned in the right hand. The slack right hand does in fact help the left in controlling the stick, but not actively. When the ball is played, the right hand must be tight on the stick, so that the ball can be moved better. Without changing the position of the feet at all, the ball should now be moved across the body, along a line parallel to the shoulders, until level with the left foot. At that point it is stopped on the reverse stick. To make a correct stop, the stick must be turned by the left hand alone, as described above. If the right hand is gripping the stick too firmly and prevents it from turning freely, the reverse stick stop cannot be carried out properly. Care should also be taken to see that, in the course of the reverse stick stop, the blade is in vertical position, level with the left foot, sooner than the ball; it must be already in position waiting for it. After the reverse stick stop in front of the left foot, the ball is played back with the reverse stick towards the right foot where it is stopped in the orthodox manner after the left hand has turned the stick again.

The next methodical step is to play the ball from the right foot to the left and back again but without stopping it at all. The body should slightly follow the movements of ball and stick; body, stick and ball should act as a unit. The ball should not pass too close in front of the feet but far enough away from the body to keep the arms well outstretched. Only when the player manages to twist the stick with the left hand and to let it slip around in the right, will he prevent his forearms from being crossed; a mistake caused by the wrong functions of both hands!

Only when these preliminary exercises, with the participants stationary, have been thoroughly mastered, so that the movements can be carried out quickly, can the coach now get them to walk, and then run slowly, controlling the ball in front of the body and alternating the reverse stick and forehand. Again, the body should 'swing' to follow the movements of stick and ball.

The last steps in learning the Indian style of dribbling are dribbling practices at speed through lines of flags, or around a circle, square (*Fig. 5*) or triangle. First, players move in one direction only. Secondly, two players start simultaneously from opposite ends, so that they meet in the middle. Finally, players run down the field about eight metres apart, working in combination (with first one and then two balls per pair). Whilst dribbling both forehand and with reverse stick, they should pass suddenly to the partner running level with them.

Looking up from the ball while dribbling

The Asians are still today the masters where dribbling is concerned. A top-player dribbling the ball is able to survey the general state of the play at any given moment and sum it up, because he knows how to look up from the ball while dribbling. The majority of European players, because of their lack of flair and insufficient technique, have to concentrate too much on the ball, with the result that they find difficulty in keeping their bearings and many tactical opportunities are missed. As *Fig. 8* shows, a player's peripheral vision is quite sufficient for watching the ball. The greater this field of indirect vision the more favourable are the conditions for a good overall view of the

Fig. 8. Harbinder Singh of India looking up from the ball while dribbling against Ceylon in the 1971 Asian Games at Bangkok.

play; all the better, too, are the prospects of selecting the correct pass, from the several alternatives that the team-mates are presenting to the ball carrier of winning a duel with a defender, for the attacker can, even when dribbling, keep a close eye on his opponent and take appropriate evasive action against intended tackles.

Raising the eyes from the ball as often as possible while dribbling must be placed on the training programme of all top-class players. Training must be built up in such a way that the player, while controlling the ball, learns how to look down only for essential actions, for instance when taking the ball, at the moment of passing or while actually shooting at goal.

Methodical series of drills for learning how to look up from the ball while dribbling:
1. The players line up as for the three player exercise (*Fig. 2*) and practise orthodox dribbling. The following suggestions from the coach should be heeded:
a) The player must learn not to incline the upper part of the body too far forwards (*Fig. 1a*) and to keep the ball far enough away from the body to maintain the widest possible field of vision (*Fig. 8*).
b) While dribbling over distances of 22.90m, the player should look up five

13

times, then ten times and finally as often as possible from the ball, to look at his partner, who stands opposite.
c) When keeping the ball continually in contact with the curve, the player should be aware of his opponent's stick so that he can move the ball with a quick wrist movement to the side or push or flip it forward to avoid an opponent's tackle.
d) The player dribbling has to increase or decrease his speed according to signals from the coach who positions himself outside the practice area. The coach holds, for instance, a stick vertically to denote an increase in pace, horizontally for a decrease.
e) The players are given the job of calling out, as they dribble, the number of fingers clearly shown by the raised hand of their partners who stand opposite them.

2.
a) Two teams are divided into two groups, which face each other diagonally 22.90m apart, their path cutting across that of their opponents (*Fig. 9*). The first player of each team dribbles the ball on the front stick or also alternatively with forehand and reverse over to the other group of his own players, gives the ball to the next player and joins on at the end of the line.
b) Competition: The winning team is the one to return to its original formation first.
c) Four balls are used simultaneously instead of two. Because the first players in all four groups now have to dribble the ball over to the groups opposite, they are compelled to look up while dribbling and to use in the precise moment a forehand or reverse stick touch to avoid a collision. Because of the real danger of injury which could be caused by collisions, this practice should not be competitive.
c) As in a). Each team reverts to one ball. This time, instead of dribbling the ball to the group opposite, the first player is met in the middle (i.e. after

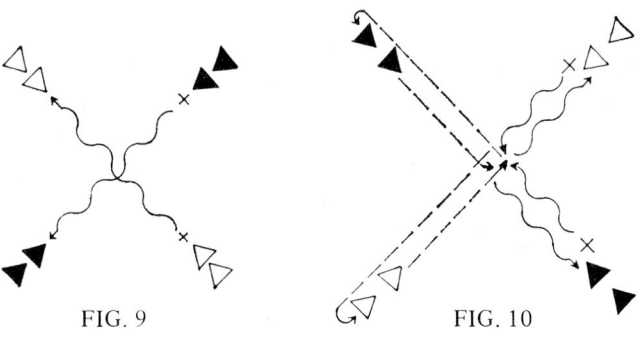

FIG. 9   FIG. 10

about 10m) by a player running towards him from the other group. The ball is transferred to this other player and the first player, who has just given up the ball, completes the remaining 10m to the opposite group, where he joins on at the back of the line. The other player, after taking over the ball, dribbles it to the second player in the original group and he proceeds in exactly the same way as the first player did (*Fig. 10*).

3. In a square (6m × 6m) ten to fourteen players are each given a ball to dribble; they must never stand still and they are to avoid touching any other player or ball.
4. Two playing areas, as in 3 above, are marked off some 22.90m apart. The same number of players dribble a ball in each area with the same aim as in 3 above. When the coach gives the signal, all the players have to dribble their ball into the other playing area, where they then continue to dribble as in the previous practice until the coach gives the next signal. Which team manages to get all its players into the other playing area first? No contact with another player or ball is to take place either while dribbling in the playing area or when changing places. Warn players about the risk of injury from collisions.
5. Two players, each with a ball, stand 3m apart, one behind the other. The rear man must copy every action made by the front man as he dribbles (e.g. dribbling along a straight line, off to a side, on a zig-zag course or with sudden changes of speed).
6. 'Cops and Robbers'
One 'robber' dribbles the ball between the centre and 22.90m line and tries to shake off two other players ('cops') following him, 3m behind, each with a ball, by changes of direction. How long will it take the 'cops' without losing control of their balls, to touch the robber's ball?

Tactics in dribbling

Dribbling has varied in importance in the course of the game's history. At the turn of the century it had its heyday but with changes in team formation (see 'The Development of Team Formations' page 171) and the arrival of close inter-passing, which stemmed from these changes, dribbling has declined in importance. Although dribbling is no longer a predominant feature of the modern game — it slows the game down and requires unnecessary strength and concentration — there are nonetheless frequent situations, in which dribbling becomes absolutely necessary for tactical considerations.

1. When a forward has broken clear of all the defence and the way to the opponent's goal is free, he has to dribble the ball. If there is still quite a considerable way to go to goal, the forward should keep the ball reason-

ably far in front of him, so that he can maintain the best speed possible. If, however, an opponent — especially the goalkeeper — is close, the ball must be kept as near to the stick as possible.

As a defender running without the ball is generally faster than a forward dribbling, the dribbler can frequently gain some advantage by so altering his course to make it coincide with that of his pursuer. By this means he will hinder the defender in his running and attempts to tackle. This tactical stratagem should only be employed, of course, if the pursuing opponent is very close and the forward is not going to succeed in obtaining a sufficient lead by a quick burst. (See pages 90-92.)

2. If the opposition has kept up a steady pressure on your defence, a defender should not immediately just hit the ball aimlessly upfield when he gains possession but, where no danger of losing the ball to a close opponent exists, should try to keep the ball for a while to give his own side a little breathing space. In addition, keeping possession of the ball on the front stick at the right side of the body allows your own side to form up again for an attack.

3. It often occurs that the ball cannot be passed on immediately, because your own players are being too closely marked or because they consider it unnecessary to run into the open spaces. In this case the player in possession should keep the ball close to the stick and dribble forward or, even better, across the field. The reason for this is that, by dribbling in this way, he will make his own players aware of the need for running into the open spaces.

When dribbling diagonally across the field, the dribbler must look up as often as possible from the ball to register the positions of his own side so as to be able to find someone to pass to at the earliest favourable opportunity.

4. Another occasion when dribbling can prove valuable is when a forward has already run off-side. Then the player in possession should not get rid of the ball, but should continue to dribble until the player has got back on-side again.

From this it is evident that modern hockey — which depends essentially on inter-passing — cannot entirely do without the dribble, despite certain limitations.

3 The Push Strokes

In direct contrast with the hit, the push is mostly used for passing over short distances. Beginners should be instructed in pushing from the very first coaching session, after they have first assimilated the basic principles of dribbling as the push is the quickest and easiest of all the methods of passing to learn.

The complete movement of the push is relatively simple compared with the other ways of passing i.e. the hit, the flick and the scoop. It takes far less time and is carried out without much preliminary action. Using a pushed pass, the player dribbling can play the ball at any moment in any direction even when dribbling at top speed.

Just as with the hit, the player should generally place himself sideways-on to the push, so that his left shoulder points in the intended direction of the pass. The feet are a shoulder's width apart, the legs are not straight and the trunk is inclined forwards. The left hand takes hold of the stick from the left or from above, and grips it at the top of the handle (the left hand should be on a level with the left knee), while the right hand is brought round onto the stick from the right and holds it in the middle. The ball, placed level with the left heel in a comfortable distance in front of the body, should be played with the lowest part of the straight handle just at the beginning of the curve. Because the face of the stick is placed directly behind the ball, the backswing is dispensed with and so, too, the crack of stick hitting ball is missing on impact.

The push stroke results from an explosive and lightning quick whipping action of the right arm towards the left. However, in order to be in a position to give a good, hard pushed pass, it is absolutely necessary for the player, before pushing, to adopt a comfortable side-on position, with the weight firmly placed on the right (or back) foot (for functional reasons this has to be avoided when pushing out the ball during a penalty corner). Simultaneously with the action of wrists and forearms, there takes place a shift of weight from the right leg, which is bent, onto the left foot; in so doing the right leg is straightened because of the quick, powerful thrust as the weight is finally transferred.

At first many players find difficulty in pushing the ball any great distance, because they cannot co-ordinate exactly enough the movement of the arms and the shift of weight from one foot to the other. However, when they do learn to transfer the weight of the body and, at the same time, to apply the

Fig. 11a and Fig. 11b. Fernandez (India) pushes the ball out for a penalty corner in the 4th World Cup in Bombay in 1982 against Holland.

muscle power of the arms and the shoulders to the stick, they will certainly be able to push the ball the width of the field.

At the end of the push stroke the stick should follow through after the ball as far as possible, so as to keep better control over it and thus obtain maximum accuracy of direction (*Fig. 12*). If, however, immediately after the shift in weight and the actual push stroke, which are both aimed in the same direction, the direction of the stick face following through after the ball, is swiftly changed to the left or right, the opponent can easily be deceived by thus concealing the direction of the push and will have great difficulty in recognising the passer's real intentions (see 'Disguising the direction of the hit' page 61 and *Fig. 13*).

The push should also be carried out from a frontal position (see *Fig. 14* page 24) when necessary. As it is then not possible to put the weight of the player's body to any real advantage and as the room available for the full use of the arms is also severely restricted, maximum power cannot be developed with a pushed pass made from this position.

The pushed pass from a frontal position is generally much less accurate than one from the side-on position, as the position of the body impedes ball control. Despite this, every player should master this pass, particularly as he will not always have the time in a game to get into a side-on position when trying to push to his front.

For the practice of the pushed pass from the frontal position or a 'bowling' hit from the frontal position the same exercises can be used as for the push

Fig. 12. a perfect illustration of the push stroke by the Indian Amarjit. Note the position of the hands and the follow through to obtain maximum accuracy of direction

from a side position. Care should be taken that the isolated skill is always practised in the context in which the skill occurs during play.

Methodical series of exercises for the pushed pass

1. Pushing the ball around a triangle. After the push the player always moves to an overlapping position beyond the player he passes to, in case four players are involved in the practice.
2. Three players push the ball to each other. The player receiving the ball indicates to his partner by his position where he would like the ball to be passed (to his reverse side or to his front stick). Practice passing around the triangle in both directions.
3. Practising accurate pushes in pairs. The players must attempt to push the ball within the confines of a narrow lane (e.g. between two adjacent pitches) or along the sideline itself, with an intermediate running free.
4. Passing competition: two pairs of players stand opposite each other behind two lines marked out 12m apart. In the middle, between them, two cones are placed 1m apart. In a set period of time the players attempt to push the ball through the goals as many times as possible. The pair scoring the most goals within the prescribed time is the winner. As a variation, each player can also play his partner in order to decide the contest. Who will be the first to score ten goals? The winners can have another round, while the losers for their part can discover a consolation prize winner. Try the same exercise in a triangle with three players and two goals.
5. Pushing relay practice: There are four players in each team. The two halves of the team stand 10m to 20m apart. Each player must make a pushed pass (from the side-on position) and then run after the ball and join the line-up opposite. Which team produces twenty pushed passes first or which team produces the most pushes in two minutes?
6. The ball is placed to the right of the back foot just in front of the body. After moving the ball to the left to bring it in front of the left foot the ball, still rolling slowly, is pushed to one's partner.
7. The ball is moved from the side-on position past the left (or front) foot along the intended line of the pass, overtaken by means of a chainstep (as if jumping out to drive in cricket) — left — right — left and then pushed to one's partner at the moment the left foot comes down for the second time and the left shoulder is pointing at the partner.
8. To learn the push while running at full speed, the ball has to be moved four to six metres away by the player himself. The player runs quickly after the ball, then, immediately before the push, he swings round from

the frontal position to get into the necessary side-on position to the ball and pushes it to his partner, when the left foot comes to the front again. As variation the player should be asked to execute the push also from a frontal position on the right and left foot.

9. Relay Practice: The first player dribbles the ball from the centre line to the 22.90m line. After running round a cone there, he pushes the ball, from there, back to the next player, who is waiting beyond the centre line. If the push is so weak that it fails to reach the line of players, the original player must run after it and push it a second time. On no account must the player waiting to receive the ball go into the area between the centre line and the 22.90m line, before the ball has crossed the line.
10. Who can push the ball, which is placed three paces away, furthest?
11. 'Chase the ball': Practise chasing the ball across the width of the field between the centre line and the 22.90m line with two teams of three. Wherever the ball is stopped, a pushed pass must be made towards the opponent's end of the playing area. The point of the game is to push the ball over the far line (the side line). If the ball goes over either of the 'touch lines' (the centre or 22.90m line), then it must be pushed back into play by the opposite side at the point at which it went over the line.

Fig. 13. Disguising a push pass demonstrated by Michael Peter (West Germany) in a test match against England.

The winning side is either the one scoring the most points in a set period of time or the one scoring a set number of points first.

Variation: More skilful players could be granted only two touches of the ball to increase the momentum of the drill and encourage stronger control.

12. Pushing as in 7 to 10 above: But this time the right foot should be brought forward at the moment of impact.
13. Pushing on the run, to both left and right; this practice is done to a partner running level and parallel 10m away.
14. Four players run continously between the centre and the 22.90m line. One of them is in possession of the ball which he has to deliver (when given the name of one of his team mates) as fast as possible with a push. The receiving players always have to signal where they want to receive the pass.
15. Three against one (two) in a square. Attempt to achieve ten push passes before the defender can intercept. As variation restrict the ball contact to two touches.

4 Stopping and Receiving

Stopping the ball without rebound or on a higher level receiving it without trapping it deadly in order to initiate immediately the next move is a prerequisite for a good game of hockey and a good personal performance depends on it. Stopping and receiving are skills which very few players manage to master completely, because to absorb the ball's speed and control it so that it stays at the end of the stick without bouncing off too far, or receive it in a way that an immediate second play at the ball is possible, demands considerably great skill.

Any unsureness in receiving is not only attributable to mistakes of technique and lack of footwork when trying to get into the correct position, but is also frequently caused by concentrating insufficiently on the approaching ball. Stopping and receiving is a test, therefore, of both skill and concentration. It is often to be noticed, especially among young players, that their thoughts, even while they are in the process of executing the stop, have already turned to the problem of beating the opponent, having a shot at goal or making the next pass. The result of this 'next step' thinking is that the passer achieves to select the right method of receiving but the act of stopping the ball lacks the necessary care and, above all, concentration, so that the ball is not brought under control. A good hockey player must be able to stop a ball hit from any direction at speeds which vary enormously.

Thus he has to estimate not only the speed of the approaching ball but also have sufficient speed, mobility and skill at his disposal to enable him to get his body and stick quickly into the desired position. The faster the ball, the quicker the player must get the stick behind the approaching ball to bring it under control. For the person receiving the ball, the stopping of inaccurate passes makes particular demands on his speed, mobility and skill, while an accurate pass is relatively easy to control.

Quite independently of whether the ball is relatively difficult or easy to reach, the player must then attempt to take the approaching ball, even in a difficult situation, so as to be able to use it again quickly without time being wasted teeing it up. The prompt passing on of the ball is only possible, however, if the player receiving the ball has already checked up on the position of his own side and of his opponents before he receives it. The modern hockey player observes the old tactical instruction 'stop, then look' in reverse. The speed of the game now demands this.

Very good players should be able to feint with movements of the body while receiving the ball. If a feint is carried out before the ball is received, considerable advantages can often be derived.

The stop can be divided up into various different aspects. According to the position of the player to the ball, we differentiate between stopping to the front and to the side; and according to the height of the approaching ball, between low, medium and high balls. But we could also add as possible divisions: stopping while standing and while running as well as stopping on the forehand and reverse side.

Stopping on the forehand

There are three possible ways of stopping the ball in a frontal position:

1. Stopping the ball to the front on natural grass with the stick in a vertical position (*Fig. 14*). During a stop to the front (with the shoulders to the front and legs comfortably apart) the weight of the body is evenly distributed on both bent legs with the knees inclined forward in order to guarantee that the trunk stays almost upright which allows good vision for the next move. The left hand grips the stick from above (see 'Indian style of dribbling' page 9), so that looking downwards the player stopping will not be able to see his left thumb. Only the correct position of the left hand will allow the player to move the stick and later the ball in the desired direction. In addition the left hand should incline the stick a little forwards towards the ball to avoid the possibility of the ball bouncing off the head of the stick. Keeping the right hand slack will also make sure that the ball does not rebound from the stick. Furthermore, while stopping, one must take care to see that the left forearm forms an almost straight line with the stick, and is not bent at the left wrist. The right hand grips in the middle of the stick or even a little lower. In fact, the lower the right hand is, the easier it is to move the stick quickly to the ball.

Fig. 14. P. Caninenberg of Germany getting right behind the ball – the safest way of stopping it

The ball is stopped in front of the body, directly beneath the player's eyes, with the stick in a completely vertical position on natural grass or on artificial turf in case the oncoming ball bounces.

Besides necessitating an accurate assessment of the speed and direction of the ball, stopping to the front demands quick, skilful footwork. That alone allows the player to adjust his position in relation to the ball in such a way that it is properly 'in his sights'. (See Exercise no. 3.)

2. On artificial turf the whole flat face of the stick is used for stopping the ball. Instead of being held vertically the stick is now placed horizontally on the ground (*Fig. 16*) so that the knuckles of the right hand have contact with the ground. Care should be taken that both legs are

Fig. 15. The basic position shown by Olympic silver medalist (1984) Ulrich Hänel (West Germany – left half)

Fig. 16. Receiving in front of the body on the front stick, with the eyes in line with the oncoming ball

Fig. 17. Receiving should always be a part of the continuation of the game, as seen here when the left wing controls the ball on the front stick, before giving an effective pass on the run

completely bent when stopping to ensure an upright trunk and therefore sufficient vision for the next move. Only when the oncoming ball bounces slightly should it be stopped with the stick in a vertical position placed exactly beside the foot which in the moment of stopping is advanced.

3. The player waiting for a pass from the right or left expects the ball with his feet in a striding position. The feet are at right angles to the line of the approaching ball, the pelvis is parallel to the line of the approaching ball, and the trunk is turned to the right through 90° towards the ball, so that the upper part of the body has to be twisted round in order to receive the ball (see *Fig. 17*).

Exercises:

1. Two players stand 4m apart, face to face, in the basic position. They play the ball to each other in such a way that the receiver stops it between his feet with the stick in a vertical position and pushes it back using the frontal position. The position of the feet must be altered if the ball arrives too far to the left or right.

2. Two players, standing 6-8m apart, hit the ball deliberately inaccurately to the left or right of the other player. By dint of quick positioning before stopping, the receiver should always stop the ball in the frontal position. Stopping on the reverse stick side should not be brought in with this drill.
3.
a) Three players stand 4m apart on the side line of the field; a passer stands in front of them about 15m away. The passer plays the ball to player no. 1, who, after a stop to the front, passes the ball back. Then the ball is passed back to player no. 2 and so on. When the passer has played the ball to the last player in the line, the competition, in which other groups of similar ability take part for purposes of comparison, is completed.
b) Variation: When the passer has played the ball to the last man in the line, he joins the end of the line while the last player with the ball takes over as passer (see *Fig. 18*).

   The competition is over when each player has had one turn as passer.
c) Variation: instead of a relay practice with the players in line abreast, a relay with the players in single file can also be formed as in *Fig. 19*. After each return to the passer, the front man goes to the end of the line. Which group gets its first player back to the head of the line first? Or, if an accurately passed ball is not stopped by the player, he has to fall out of line. Who is the last player left in?
4. A difficult drill is a circular relay using two balls. Four players, spaced about 10m apart, form a circle, facing inwards. In the middle of the circle is a passer using two balls. He passes one ball accurately to player no. 1 and, directly afterwards, the second ball to player no. 2 (see *Fig. 20*). Meanwhile he receives the first ball back from player no. 1 and he im-

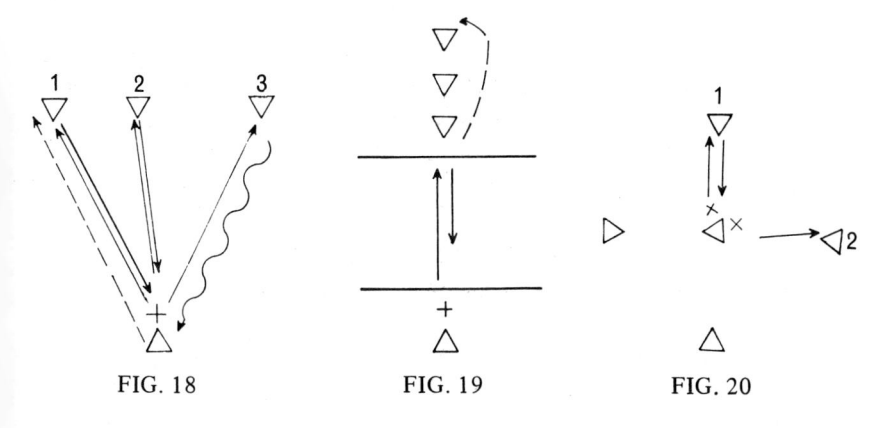

FIG. 18   FIG. 19   FIG. 20

mediately passes it to player no. 3. This continues until the last player in the circle has received the ball. Care must be taken to see that this drill starts very slowly but, with increasing sureness, the tempo can be raised.

A competitive element can be introduced by forming a second circle of players.

5. Competition with hits: two players face each other at a distance of 22.90m, standing in goals of 10-12 metres width. The aim is to score the most goals from free hits. (The ball must not leave the ground.)

Stopping the ball on natural grass to the side is, by comparison with taking the ball to the front, much less certain to succeed. Because the ball is not properly in the receiver's 'sights', but is moving to the side of the body, it is difficult to follow and assess as accurately its direction and speed. A poor stop frequently results from the fact that the ball is not travelling directly along the player's line of sight.

On really flat pitches, as for instance on artificial turf or indoors, the extra footwork required to bring the player into the frontal position is not necessary, so that the side-on stopping, with the stick parallel to the ground, is the most usually favoured method of taking the ball. This, in contrast to frontal stopping, allows the receiver to analyse the exact position of his opponent marking him and to act according to his behaviour.

When forwards are closely marked by the opposing defenders, the ability to stop to the side, becomes a tactical must. If the ball is passed from behind to an unmarked forward (either from the right or left hand side), he should, in order to avoid obstructing when receiving the ball, stop the ball, not in a frontal position with his back to the man marking him, but to the side or even with his back towards the passer. In the latter case, which is to be seen relatively rarely, the toes of the forward point in the direction he will take to goal and the head and shoulders are moved towards the side from which the ball is coming, so that he is able to follow it carefully.

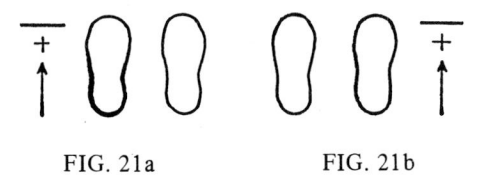

FIG. 21a   FIG. 21b

At the same time, the stick-face is placed towards the direction from which the ball is coming. If it reaches the forward on the left hand side, it will be stopped on the forehand but facing backwards (*Fig. 21a*); if it arrives on the right hand side of the attacker, it is stopped on the reverse stick (*Fig. 21b*). With this method of taking the ball, which involves twisting the body round, the ball is not always to be stopped dead. For tactical reasons, it is sometimes better merely to take the pace off the ball – with the player who is making for his opponent's goal adjusting his running speed to the speed of the approaching ball – in such a way that taking the ball can be translated without delay into a dribble at top speed leaving the surprised opponent standing.

To avoid obstructing while taking the ball, the very closely marked forward should be expected, therefore, to be able to stop to the side or, even better, to run to the ball in order to get away from the opponent at the same time collecting the ball to the side (see: 'Tactical considerations before or whilst taking the ball' page 35); a defender on the other hand or the wing with the side line of the field at his back should prefer as far as possible, to use the less risky frontal stop.

All the exercises already mentioned for stopping on the forehand to the front can also be used, by means of a slight change in position – i.e. moving sideways to the ball – for learning to take the ball to the side. Further drills for practising the stop will be introduced in connection with the reverse stick stop.

The reverse stick stop

Nowadays the reverse stick stop has become just as important as stopping to the right, and in some positions of the field (inside forwards and midfield players) has gained even more importance because of the possibility to pass the ball which came from behind, immediately. In earlier days it was avoided as much as possible and players were sometimes even stopped from using it on the grounds of the player's lack of technique and also because of the long blade which made it difficult to turn the stick over quickly. Nowadays, however, the beginner must grasp the reverse stick stop right from the start of his hockey career. A young player's skill and his ability to learn are not the only factors in favour of doing so. If the young player masters the reverse stick stop from the beginning, he will then avoid turning the body unnecessarily when taking the ball; in early practice games this could otherwise lead to frequent obstructions and thereby to injuries as well.

The traditional reverse stick stop in the side-on position can be executed in two possible ways:

1. The stick is held in the Indian dribbling position, that is: the right hand grips it loosely in the middle whilst the stick is being turned; the left hand grips rather more firmly coming from above onto the handle right at the top. The right shoulder of the player points towards the approaching ball. So that the ball, when passed from the right, does not hit the

back of the stick, the left hand has to turn the stick through 180° anti-clockwise, the right hand being left slack. Thus the stick head describes a semicircle above the moving ball. Only if the flat side of the stick is now facing the ball after the turn through 180°, with the toe pointing to the ground, can the reverse stick stop succeed.

To avoid the ball jumping upwards (if stopped level with the right foot) or bouncing off (if stopped midway between the feet), the ball should run past the body until level with the left foot, before it is stopped. The reason being that, if the stick is level with the left foot during the stop, the face is slightly inclined towards the right, thus reducing the chances of the ball bouncing off. The player should note the position of his hands on the stick when he has successfully stopped a ball level with his left foot in this way. The back of the right hand should be pointing to the right and the back of the left hand should, at this stage, be pointing downwards.

However, as the player can develop only very little power with the left hand gripping underneath the handle in this manner, he is frequently all too easily dispossessed after a reverse stick stop, especially when the left hand alone is holding the stick. To prevent this and to make it possible for the player to produce an effective pass immediately after this stop, it is advisable for him to let the left hand slide round to the right, so that the back of the hand now points to the left. This grip alone will guarantee the transmission of full power from the arm to the stick thus permitting effective reverse stick play.

2. The position of the player in relation to the ball is the same as in the first example of the reverse stick stop. But this time the fingertips of the right hand alone are turning the stick face clockwise. The grip of both hands is kept slack. The fingertips of the right hand turn the stick.

One must distinguish the different movements of the stick face as it goes to meet the ball when using either of the two methods of reverse stick stop. In the first method the left hand alone leads the anti-clockwise movement of the curve *over the* ball; in the second method, the right fingertips alone lead the clockwise movement of the curve between ball and feet.

As this variation of grip during the reverse stick stop allows the stick face to be placed much more quickly behind the ball, it is used especially for stopping the hard hit ball and for taking short distance passes. In the interests of methodical coaching, however, the beginner should initially only be shown the normal reverse stick stop (see the first example). It can be taught without any great difficulty, once he has mastered the Indian type of dribbling.

The two techniques of stopping the ball with the reverse stick on natural grass mentioned above apply in the main also to hockey on artificial turf. However, because of the lack of bounce, stationary stops should be made with the stick laid down horizontally on the ground, using the whole flat surface for stopping (*Fig. 22*). When using this kind of reverse stick stopping there are some important points to take into consideration:

1. The stick should be held in the left hand only with the knuckles (some players tape them) touching the ground. This way it will be more comfortable and quicker to get the stick into a horizontal position.
2. Care should be taken that the player bends his knees sufficiently (femur and tibia almost form a right angle with the right knee lower than the left one) in order to allow quick movements immediately after stopping and good vision. The centre of gravity whilst stopping remains between the feet, which means better balance.
3. The stick should be placed perpendicular to the path when stopping with the reverse. When receiving the ball from the right it should be angled to the path of the ball in order to reduce the force of the pass acting on the stick and to let the ball rebound across the body to the forehand side.
4. The stop should be made towards the middle of the stick, better closer to the left hand than to the curve of the stick.

Fig. 22. Which three mistakes are carried out in this figure? The text above will give the answers!

Exercises for practising the reverse stick stop with the player stationary

1.
a) Two players face each other approximately sixteen metres apart. One of them has a ball. Between them a third player positions himself in such a way that his right shoulder always points in the direction of the player in possession (*Fig. 23*). Whereas the outside players always pass the ball to the player in the middle from the normal position and stop it to the front on the forehand, the player in the middle stops the pass on the reverse stick side using one of the three techniques mentioned above and then passes the ball, from the same position, to his left.

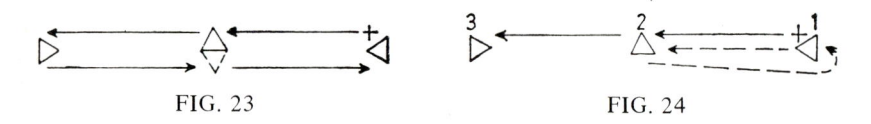

FIG. 23   FIG. 24

b) The same drill with several three man groups. Which middle player stops the ball on the reverse stick side most frequently within the space of two minutes?

In addition in this drill, the stick face shall only be turned towards the ball when the pass has actually been given by the outside player. When this drill is carried out at speed, there is no break between stopping and passing.

c) As in a). After the reverse stick stop, the player in the middle feints to give a reverse stick pass to the right (back to the passer) by pulling the toe of the stick along the ground towards the right but keeping it in front of the ball. The ball now lies between stick and body by means of this piece of stick deception; it is therefore hidden from his opponent and temporarily out of his range. The effect gained by this stick deception is reinforced by a slight shift of weight from the left foot onto the right and, immediately afterwards, the player in the middle sweeps the ball to the left instead with the stick in the normal position.

d) As in a). The middle player ceases to alter his position in relation to each passer. Thus he stops the first ball on the reverse stick side and then gives a forehand pass, but takes the return ball with the front stick to give a reverse stick pass and so on.

e) The same with several groups of three to form a competition. Which middle player produces the greatest number of reverse stick stops in the space of two minutes? These are to be counted out aloud by the player himself.

f) As in d). The player in the middle feints to pass the ball, after every stop, to the side from which it has just come.
g) The same arrangement as in d). After the first pass to the player in the centre, the players change places as follows: player no. 1 passes to player no. 2 and immediately runs to take no. 2's place (*Fig. 24*). Player no. 2 stops the ball, plays it on to no. 3 and runs to the position vacated by player no. 1 and so on. Thus, when a player finds himself in the middle, he must always run off in the opposite direction to the ball after giving his pass, whereas the players at each side must run after the ball into the middle.
2. Circles, each made up of six players, are formed. The space between each individual player should be about 6m. Each circle has one ball which one player passes to his left to the next player on the coach's command. When passing with the forehand special attention must be paid that the ball is being passed to the next player about 1m in front of his body onto the reverse stick side. The winning group is the circle in which the ball is returned first to the original passer. The game can be made more exciting if the ball has to go round the circle, two, three or four times.

The following rules must be observed in this competition.
— Every player must take his turn in passing.
— If the ball is stopped on the forehand instead of on the reverse stick, the stopper must return the ball to the passer.
— If a player fails to bring a pass under control with the reverse stick, it must be retrieved by the same player and passed on from his designated position on the circle line.

Variation: The game can be played with two or more balls. Only when all the balls have returned to the original players shall a halt be called.
3.
a) The players stand opposite each other two metres apart. Each then

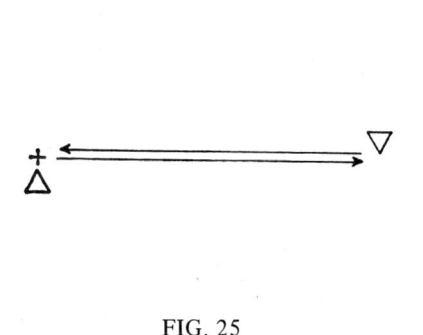

FIG. 25   FIG. 26

moves three paces to his left (*Fig. 25*). One player executes a firm reverse stick pass, to the other player who stops it on the reverse stick side and also returns the ball with a reverse stick pass. When passing with reverse stick the right arm is at full stretch gripping the stick in the centre with the hook pointing down to the ground, so that the back of the left hand points to the left and the back of the right towards his partner.

b) As before. This time, however, before each reverse stick pass is made with the ball stationary, the player moves the ball to and fro, a few times, in front of the body, as if dribbling Indian style (e.g. forehand – reverse stick – forehand – reverse stick pass).

4. Two players stand facing each other, 10m apart. One pushes the ball so accurately to his partner that it travels along the line of the partner's left foot. The player waiting for the ball stands facing it at first but, when he is sure that the ball really is coming to him on the left hand side, he turns his body through 90° to the left (*Fig. 26*). To carry out this turn, the player has to pivot round on the ball of his right foot, and the left foot is placed behind the right, so that they are a shoulder's width apart. When in this position the player's right shoulder should be pointing at the passer. This quarter turn of the body is accompanied by a turn of the stick either with the left hand (as in the first method) or with the right (as in the second method). The ball is stopped level with the left foot. After the reverse stick stop, the ball can then be taken right round the body, with the player turning to adopt a side-on position facing to the right (the left shoulder now pointing towards his partner) before pushing the ball back from the normal side on position.

Drills for practising the reverse stick stop on the run:

1. After establishing eye contact, player no. 1 gives a square pass to the left for player no. 2 to run onto (*Fig. 27*); the latter must control the ball in one of the following ways depending on the speed of the pass or the speed of his own approach to the ball. If he reaches the ball easily, he receives it on the front stick with his feet in the striding position (right or left foot forwards – see example no. 3 (page 26, and *Fig. 17*) of stopping in the frontal position.

    If he is unable to get his body into the line of the ball, he must stop it on the reverse stick, either with two hands or with one hand only, depending on how far he is from the ball. When player no. 2 has definitely got the ball under control, he returns it after eye contact to player no. 3, who is standing on his right, with a forehand pass if he has stopped it on front stick and with a reverse stick pass, if he had taken it on the reverse stick side. After giving his return pass each player goes to the back of the other group. Care should be taken that the ball is always controlled whilst still running, a necessity of modern attacking hockey. When receiving the ball on the run, the player should try to make maximum use of the surface of the stick.

2. The first player after establishing eye-contact with his team-mate gives a square pass for player no. 2 to run onto and which the latter stops on the reverse stick (*Fig. 28*). The moment no. 2 makes contact with the ball, player no. 3 runs forward to take the square pass given by no. 2. After giving their passes, players nos. 1 and 2 run diagonally across to the other group and join on at the back. There should be ten to twelve metres between players nos. 1 and 3 at the beginning of this drill.

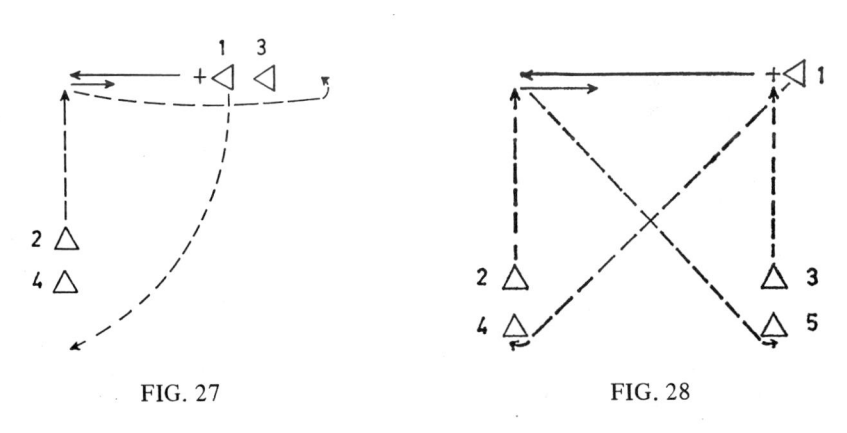

FIG. 27   FIG. 28

Tactical considerations before or whilst receiving the ball

In these days of tight marking and covering, attackers can really only gain possession of the ball without causing some infringement when they learn after establishing eye-contact with the team mate how to detach themselves from the player marking them at the precise moment that the pass intended for him is given.

The ability to know when to run towards the ball is an important tactical requirement which is still too little heeded in hockey today. Players are usually inclined to wait for the ball to come to them rather than run towards it. Although forwards, above all, have seen enough times how difficult they can make defence for their opponents if only they try running towards the ball, they nonetheless adopt a largely passive role when taking the ball.

Remaining passive before and while receiving the ball is a great tactical mistake, as it is always much more difficult for a defender to stop a forward already in possession than it is when meeting him at the moment that he is trying to receive the ball.

Account must also be taken of the psychological impact which the attacker can make on a defender by his attempts to run towards the ball. The attacker's self-confidence and sureness in receiving will rise in the same measure as the defender becomes more nervous and unsure, because the forward, by running to meet the ball, prevents the defender from coming into direct contact with it. If the forward waits passively for the ball to come to him, however, then he can be taken by his opponent at just the right moment. Therefore, when a 'shadowed' player aims to receive a ball on his front or reverse stick he should always run to meet the ball in the moment the passer moves the stick towards the ball and not earlier. Otherwise he gives the defender time to come close again whilst the pass is prepared or still on the way. Through constant practice, this will become an automatic reaction: beginners should be encouraged to do so from the outset.

Methodical series of drills:

1. Two players stand thirty metres apart behind a marked out line and hit the ball to each other. After establishing eye-contact with the player in possession of the ball and immediately before the ball is hit, the player receiving must run towards another line some three to four metres away from him (*Fig. 29*), in order to receive the ball with the front stick or with the reverse stick in a side-on position, indicating always in advance with the position of his stick where he wishes the ball to be passed. After receiving he returns the ball to his partner and then sprints back to his original position. Thus the ball during this practice will always be confined to the space between the inner lines.

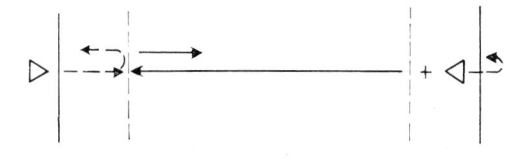

FIG. 29

2. The first drill can also be carried out with the addition of defenders, who place themselves three metres behind each of the passers. Their job is to

challenge their man when he is taking the ball on the front or the reverse stick but not actively to interfere with him. After controlling the ball, the attacker should beat the defender, dribbling the ball across the second line. In the progress of the exercise the defenders become more active.
3. As in 2, except that now both players, participate actively. While the forward tries to gain possession of the ball by running towards it, taking care not to infringe any of the rules, and then get past the defender into the circle, the defender's job is to pass the ball back to the third player on the centre line, before the forward can score.

Always when a free space exists on the right hand side of the attacker, the ball should be played preferably diagonally into this space. After controlling the ball with the reverse stick, the attacker should try to score.
4. Receive the ball in a frontal position and turn to a side position in the very last moment for facing the opponent who looks for obstructions.

Stopping at penalty corners

A penalty corner in which the two functions of stopping and hitting towards the goal are divided between two players, can be taken much more quickly, more accurately and therefore more successfully. The striker, who no longer needs to concentrate on stopping the ball with the stick, can devote his undivided attention to the shot at goal; taking up the correct position in relation to the ball even before the beginning of the shot and, above all, he can make a short approach run to the ball in order to increase the force of his shot (see 'The force of the hit' page 52).

The stickstop requires the player to move quickly into position, especially when the pass is inaccurate. The best way to stop the ball on artificial turf is with a horizontal reverse stick stop in a frontal position with the left hand behind the curve and the right hand in the middle of the handle (*Fig. 30*), or a horizontal reverse or forehand stick stop in a side-on position with both hands on the stick (see page 31).

However on natural grass and especially on bumpy fields a horizontal reverse stick stop is not recommended. Here the stopper should hold the stick completely vertical and also slightly inclined forward to stop the ball with forehand in the traditional way (see *Fig. 14*) or in the South African way (see *Fig. 31*).

Stopping the ball dead on the ground requires plenty of training and skill, above all when the advice to run towards the ball is heeded. If the stickstopper, at a penalty corner, comes a few paces into the circle immediately after the ball is hit or pushed out, he allows the player taking the corner to shoot from

Fig. 30. The German Olympic silver medal team (1984) is expecting the initial pass of the penalty corner.

Fig. 31. Stopping a penalty corner hit out on uneven grass pitches. The ball should be stopped more in front of the left foot.

38

only ten or eleven metres. The chances of scoring a goal are increased, as the reaction time for the goalkeeper and the two defenders standing on the goal-line is reduced and, in addition, the striker is given a much more favourable angle for his shot or flick.

With a rapid and smooth combination between pusher-out or hitter-out, stickstopper and striker (the best time from push-out to hit being 1 second, but still 1.5 seconds guarantees a free shot towards the goal), the defence is given very little chance, because of the time lost in starting, of reaching the ball in time, as they rush out (see 'The penalty corner' page 57).

For more information regarding the function of the striker and the stick stop during a penalty corner see page 47 'Hitting the ball on the run' and page 57 'The penalty corner'.

5 The Hit

The hit can often be of decisive importance in the outcome of a match and therefore the coach should concentrate on perfecting it. It is one of the most useful technical acquisitions for any player, of equal importance for both defenders and forwards. Its great advantage over the push and the flick lies in its endless possibilities for moving the ball quickly to any part of the pitch. The hit is made up of several components but a clear distinction is difficult between them as the hit results from a connected series of movements. In theory, the following points are of importance for carrying out a hit successfully: —
1. The position of the player in relation to the ball.
2. The grip.
3. The backswing.
4. The hit itself.

Basically, these four points must be put into practice whenever a hit is made, irrespective of whether it is made from a stationary position or on the run.

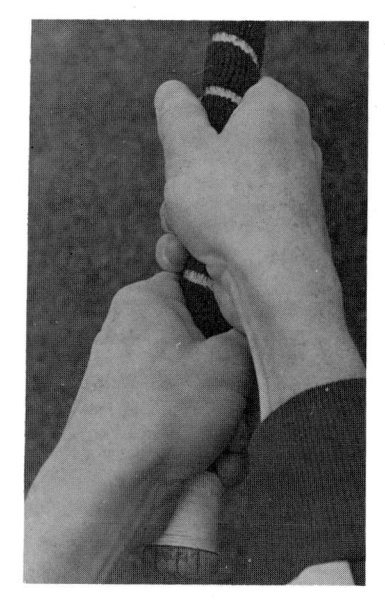

Fig. 32a, b. The grip used when hitting the ball

1. *Position of the player in relation to the ball.*

The very fact of adopting a side-on position brings together a series of factors, which are essential for a successful hit, namely: —

a) *A firm platform:*
   The player stands with legs comfortably apart, the left shoulder pointing in the direction in which the ball is to be hit (*Fig. 34*). The weight is placed equally on both feet. One must constantly check that the feet are not too close together, as near as possible to a shoulder's width apart; the feet must be firmly based in order to ensure that the player does not lose his balance while making the hit. A position with the feet any further apart should be avoided since recovery and readiness for further action is more difficult.

   With a front-on position, the platform is less firm, as only the heels support the backwards thrust of the backswing and then of the actual impact, instead of having the whole of both feet as a firm base.

   When the side-on position is adopted, the toes do not point in the direction of the intended hit; rather, in order to maintain a firm balance and to allow the weight to be transferred more easily, the toes point forwards in the same direction as the body.

b) A considerable transfer of weight from one foot to the other is made possible at the moment of impact. (See: 'The backswing' page 43 and 'The hit' page 45). When the front-on position is adopted, there is only a very slight transfer of weight from one foot to the other and therefore it is hardly possible to get any force into the hit.

c) A long backswing is made possible (see 'The backswing'). If the player adopts a front-on position the distance travelled by the backswing and the downswing is shorter than when hitting from a side-on position, so that the hit must be less powerful (see: 'The force of the hit' page 52).

   In addition, the left arm cannot be extended fully in the front-on position so that full power cannot be transferred to the ball as happens with the 'bowling' hit with the right hand in the middle of the handle.

d) *The best position visually for the ball:*
   This is afforded only by a side-on stance. When struck, the ball should be at a comfortable distance from the body, at a point between a line drawn through the centre of the body and the left foot. If the ball is level with the right foot, it is usually chopped; if it is in front of the left foot, a sliced shot results.

e) *The possibility of disguising the direction of the hit:*
   (see: 'Disguising the direction of the hit' page 61).

Fig. 33. Joginder Singh of India, like many Asians, prefers to grip the stick a little lower down when hitting the ball

For the above reasons, the player should adopt a side-on stance. The closer the player comes to a front-on stance, the more the advantages of the side-on stance already described are lost. Nevertheless, especially when there is not enough time to move into a side-on position, a hit has to be executed in a front-on position using a completely different technique which can be best described as 'bowling shot' in which the right hand leads the movement and not the left one as is the case during the hit in the side-on position.

2. *The grip.*

As soon as the player has taken up the correct position in relation to the ball, the left hand grips the stick from the left and the right hand from the right. The flat side of the stickhead points to the left and is positioned to the immediate right of the ball (*Fig. 32*).

To impart power to the hit, both hands must be together on the stick one below the other, in direct contrast to all other techniques in hockey. They should be so close to one another, that the index-finger of the upper or left hand should touch the little finger of the right or lower hand (*Fig. 32*). There are two possible positions on the handle for this grip:

a) The right hand, which grips the middle of the stick in dribbling, slides upwards until it touches the left, or upper hand. This grip is preferred especially by European players, whilst the Asians generally prefer an alternative grip.
b) Out of the dribbling position they slide the left hand down the handle, until it touches the right hand. In contrast to the first position, therefore, the upper part of the handle remains free (*Fig. 33*). As there is now a shorter grip on the stick, there is a shorter backswing. Although the hit can now be carried out more quickly, because of the smaller arc described by the stickhead, the downswing in fact must be slower than it is when using the normal grip which permits a greater speed of the stickhead. Because of the shorter backswing, there is less power in the hit. (*See* 'The force of the hit.' 2. Speed of the downswing page 53). This type of grip in no way avoids sticks, as some Asians believe. On the contrary, the Asian grip often leads to 'sticks'.

When they first pick up a hockey stick, many people grasp the end of the handle with their right hand, leaving the left hand to grip below the right. Telling a beginner that the world's best players grip the stick with the left hand uppermost, and that he must do likewise if he is to become a good player will not necessarily convince him; even a demonstration may not do so. Only a thorough explanation will convince him of the disadvantages of his right-hand-uppermost grip, and cause him to change it.

If the stick is held with the right hand at the top of the handle, neither right nor left arm can bend sufficiently to give optimal application of power and direction. The arm muscles are most efficient when the arms are half bent, when muscles are neither over-stretched or over-compressed. With a normal grip, the right hand, being further from the body, does the main work as regards power whilst the left is leading and mainly responsible for the direction. If the right hand is gripping the end of the stick, it is drawn in towards the body, and is so fully bent that an optimal transfer of power is impossible. Using that grip, a player cannot hit the ball as hard as he could with the correct grip. Another disadvantage of having the right arm drawn in to the body is that it has less freedom of movement, and directional control of the left hand is much more difficult.

3. *The backswing*

At the final point of the backswing, the stick is held as if it were an extension from the right shoulder, so that the tip points upwards. The face does not point to the ground, but is held vertically. If this is not the case, then the stickhead should be brought to a vertical position, at least until the moment of impact, in order to avoid slicing or chopping the ball. At the final point of the backswing, the stickhead should be higher than the grip of the upper hand. In order to achieve this, the right hand must move slightly (from the wrist), thumb upwards.

Both wrists are held firm! It must be emphasised that a hit is not produced solely by the action of the wrists, but depends mainly on the arms and the rotation of the right hip towards the direction of the hit (*Fig. 35*).

Because the arms play such an important part in giving speed to the stickhead and therefore in imparting power to the shot, they must remain free to move. They must not touch the body either during the backswing or at the actual moment of contact. During the backswing the right arm is slightly bent, in contrast to the left. The upper and lower arm form an angle of some $120°$ to $130°$. The right elbow, as well as the right upper arm, are therefore about a hand's breadth from the ribs (*Fig. 34*). This is a most important point and is ignored by many players.

In the backswing, the stick should never go behind the right shoulder as far to the right as to be behind a line extending from the shoulder blade. Therefore, the backswing, together with the ensuing downswing — every movement until the impact — must both be made in the vertical plane.

Fig. 34. A New Zealander about to strike the ball. Both arms will be at full stretch at the moment of contact. Former Australian captain, John McBryde, watches apprehensively.

In order to avoid any checking of the stroke the backswing and the actual downswing should be merged, as far as possible, into one movement. At the final stage of the backswing, the weight must be shifted slightly on to the right, or rear, foot, when carrying out the hit in a stationary position.

4. The hit

The actual hit begins at the highest point of the backswing. The stick pauses here for a moment between backswing and hit, and changes direction rather like a ball just as it starts to fall after being thrown vertically into the air. In order to make it easier to strike the ball, the head of the stick should already be perpendicular to the ground at that point. Between the highest point of the backswing and the point of impact the stick has to be accelerated as much as possible with the left hand leading and the right hand giving speed and direction. Attention should be paid to avoid 'sticks' when hitting through the ball. 'Sticks' after the hit is more common than before; the follow-through by stick and arms is naturally upwards and to the left unless it is checked. Actively holding back the follow-through requires that the tension produced in the muscles during the hit is not released after the impact. In

Fig. 35. Note the low positions of the hands, and the rotation of the right hip just before 'impact'.

order to hit a ball both technically faultlessly and without infringing the rules, a player needs strength not only for the hit but also for checking the follow-through too.

If the backswing and the follow-through are kept straight and are accurate in the direction of the hit, then we can generally say that the hit was well executed. But we should note that the important part of a good hit is not just the actual impact, but the backswing, the amount of momentum to the axis of the ball's travel and the check of the follow-through.

A major fault of many players is starting the downswing with his hands and arms before legs and right hip have begun to work. Compared to the action of leg and hip, the hands and the arms function passively and move as freely as possible and as fast as possible, providing they follow the lower-body actions.

Even more difficult is the hit made when on the move. As the centre of gravity moves up and down in a wavy line because the player is running, so this movement is transferred to the path followed by the stick as it goes to meet the ball. Whilst hitting on the run the player has to modify his positioning each time in relation to the ball, in order to ensure a proper impact.

Most difficult of all, however, is hitting the ball when the action of running has brought the right foot in front of the left at the moment of the hit (*Fig. 37*).

Fig. 36. Paul Litjens of the Netherlands checks his follow-through after a free hit in a Test match

Fig. 37. The author hitting off the right foot. Something that must be practised

Hitting off the right foot.
It is often impossible for an attacker to hit the ball from the best side-on position with the left foot forward, because he is about to be tackled. If there

is insufficient time to bring the left foot forward and turn the body through 90° to the right, a hit off the wrong foot may be necessary. This is made front-on to the ball, despite the disadvantates this entails. Shoulders and hips do not move in unison as is the case when hitting off the left foot, but form a right angle during the backswing (though not during the actual hit). There is then a sharp twisting of the body between hips and shoulders.

When preparing to hit off the right foot, the player straightens up only a little, and turns his shoulders 90° to the right whilst raising the stick. The left shoulder thus points where he wants the ball to go. As the right foot comes down, the ball is hit from a position in front of and slightly to the side of that foot.

A clean and accurate hit off the right foot is achieved by keeping an upright stance during both backswing and hit.

The reverse-stick hit.
The reverse-stick hit is a form of hitting off the right foot. The closer the ball is to the body in front of the right foot, the easier and harder the ball can be hit: if the ball is too far in front of the body, the stick's head has to be angled too greatly, and the hit can only be executed with the tip of the stickhead, with consequent poor transfer of strength. If the ball is close to the body, a hard hit with the beginning of the stick's head is possible, because of the perpendicular position of the stick. The grip of the stick remains the same as when hitting on the open side. Over distances greater than about 10m, the reverse-stick hit should be used only on very fast surfaces such as artificial turf. On wet grass or other slow pitches, players should preferentially pull the ball back with reverse stick (rather than *hit*) if under pressure, or hit the ball on the run after, of course, turning the left shoulder in the direction of the intended hit.

Hitting the ball on the run.
Hitting the ball on the run (e.g. when converting penalty corners) has some advantages over hitting the ball whilst stationary. When the player is running, body and stick act in unison, so that acceleration of the body is transferred to the stick. The faster a player can run towards the ball, the more the stick will be accelerated, and thus the greater will be the strength of the hit.

Hitting the ball in a technically perfect way whilst running is not, however, simple. During the run-up, the stick must be positioned so as to maximise the transfer of strength from the body and arms to the ball. Usually, the stick is raised for the hit quickly, during the penultimate step of the run-up; this reduces the player's speed. He loses further momentum because of the 90° turn to the right (from the front-on running position to the side-on hitting position). Body and stick therefore need to have gained speed early in the run-up; acceleration during the last few steps of the run-up is impossible unless the speed of the run-up is very slow indeed. The snag is that the faster a player's run-up to the ball, the less time he leaves himself for the backswing and the hit itself. So not only is the technique of hitting the ball complicated, but the chances of scoring a goal are reduced in that the stick has less time to build up momentum, and the hit cannot be as hard. Any increase in run-up speed requires a corresponding improvement in technique. An intelligent corner-striker will not approach the ball at his top speed, but rather at a compromise, medium speed. In so doing, he gives himself sufficient time to give the stick as much momentum as possible from the backswing. Reducing the speed of approach also gives him more time to take up a correct position relative to the stick stopped ball, and hit it more accurately.

Methodical series of drills: from hitting the ball when stationary to hitting the moving ball on the run.

1. Tennis forehand drive with the right hand only in a stationary position to a partner. The right hand grips the stick as described on page 42. Care should be taken that the stick moves during the backswing and the follow-through in a straight line and that the right hip before impact turns in the direction of the hit.
2. Drive with the left hand only from a stationary position to a partner. After having used both arms in the backswing, the follow-through is exclusively executed by the completely stretched left arm. Make sure the rotation of the right hip is correct.
3. Two players hit the ball to each other with both hands on the stick. The one receiving indicates to his partner, by the position of the stick, exactly where he would like to receive the ball to be hit (to his right or on his reverse stick).
4. Groups of three players are formed. The first of two of them standing behind one another hits the ball to a third, who accepts the pass about 22.90m away (*Fig. 38*); after each player has hit the ball, he runs to the other side, whilst the next player takes his place.

FIG. 38

5. The ball is placed in front of the right foot, from where it is slowly propelled to a point opposite the left heel, and, while still rolling, is hit towards the other player.

6. From the side-on position, the ball is pushed towards the left past the left (or front) foot in the direction of the intended hit. The player overtakes it with a chain step (left-right-left) and, at the moment that the left foot comes to the ground again for the second time, the ball is hit to the other player.
7. To learn to hit when running, the ball must be hit 4-6m forwards by the player himself. Running quickly after the ball, the player has to carry out a cross-step, immediately before the hit, in order to change from the frontal position to the necessary side-on position; only when the left (right) foot is forward can he then hit the ball to his partner.
8. Relay Practice: The first player dribbles the ball from the centre line to the 22.90m line. After running round a cone placed there, he hits the ball back to the next player in the line. If the hit is so weak that the ball does not reach the line of players, it must be hit again by the same player who has had to run after it. In no case may the player waiting to receive the ball go into the practice area before the ball has crossed this boundary.
9. Instead of hitting to the opposite partner the ball must be hit clockwise and also anticlockwise around a triangle (20m lines). The integrated skill of receiving and controlling the ball and hitting in a minimum of time off the left or right foot at an angle to a team mate is required as it might happen in a game.
10. The above drills are made more interesting to the players if they hit the ball to each other along a line (e.g. a side-line) or through a narrow goal, made up of two cones. Which player (team) scores the first ten goals?
11.
a) Four cones are set up to form two goals, which are each 1m wide, 22.90m apart. All four cones stand on the same line. 10(20)m behind one goal are two players (outside-rights A and B) (*Fig. 39*). A receives a ball and dribbles it, keeping parallel to the line on which all four cones stand;

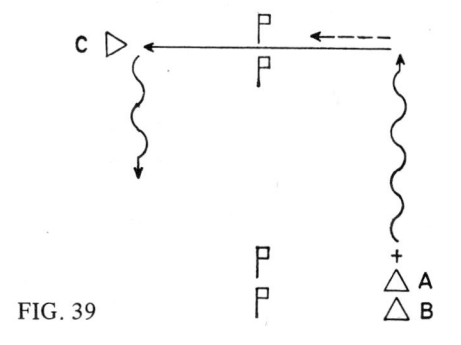

FIG. 39

when he is opposite the other goal, he hits the ball over 10(20)m, while still on the run, through the goal to a third waiting player C. The latter sets off in the same way as A. Having shot the ball through the goal, the player concerned must always follow the ball, so as to take up his new position about 10(20)m behind the goal, where he waits to receive the next player's shot.

In the course of the relay practice illustrated in *Fig. 40*, all three players act as outside-lefts and practise the very difficult hit on the run over to the right. Those players with little practice at this may be allowed to stop the ball briefly with the reverse stick before hitting to the right, whereas the more adept must hit through the goal while still on the run but without stopping the ball first.

Variation: All players expecting to receive the ball wait on the sideline of the field and run in the moment of the impact of the pass (after having established previously an eye contact with the passer) three or four metres into the field in order to collect the ball on the run.

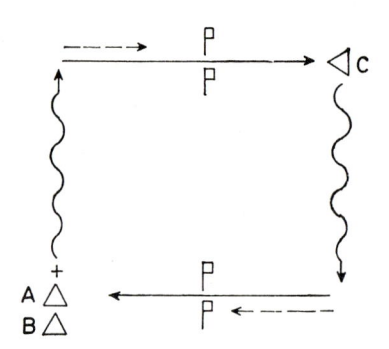

FIG. 40

b) If the practice is carried out with four players (*Fig. 41*), two of them (A and C) can set off simultaneously, each with a ball, so as to raise the tempo of the practice. It is also possible for five players to practise hitting and stopping the ball on the run.

c) When only two players are available to take part, the drill is at its simplest (*Fig. 42*). When player A has completed his dribble and hit the ball through the goal, he has to retrace his steps at full speed to get into position behind the second goal and wait for his partner's pass. Who will be the first to score ten goals? If there is too great a disparity between the two players, the size of the goals can be altered in relation to the respective abilities of the participants.

12. Player no. 1 in each line starts off dribbling at the same time as his opposite number. When they have both covered two thirds of the distance

FIG. 41

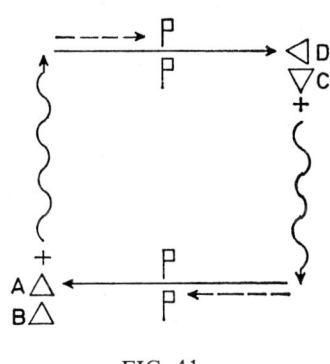

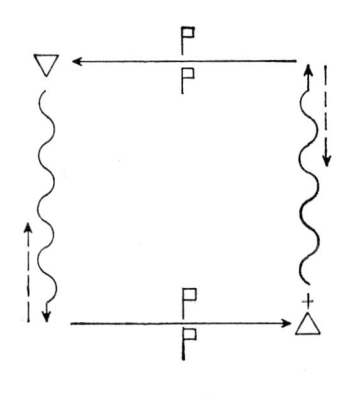

FIG. 42

(about 30m) and arrived at a point indicated by a cone, they give a moderately hit square pass (of about 20m) for the second player of the other group to run onto (*Fig. 43*). Having hit the ball on the run, the player must join the back of the other line as quickly as possible. It is important that the player, without the ball, from the opposite group does not begin to run before the player dribbling the ball has established eye-contact with him. The latter player must ensure that his pass is accurate and well timed.

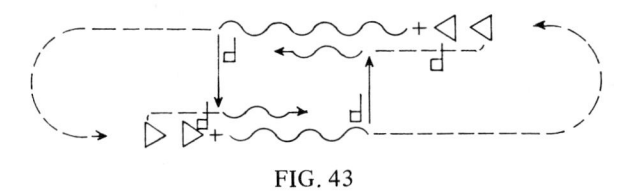

FIG. 43

13. 'Chase the ball': The idea of this game is to hit the ball over the sidelines, playing across the width of the pitch in the area bounded by the centre and 22.90m lines. After the coach has tossed up to decide which side has the first hit, the game begins with a hit from the side-line. Where the ball is finally stopped by the opponents is the point from which the next hit is taken in the opposite direction. The two sides, two to three players strong, place themselves as suitably as possible in their own half of the playing area so as to be in the best positions to intercept the ball.

If the ball goes out (i.e. over the centre or 22.90m lines), it must be hit back into play by the opposing side at the spot where it crossed the line. The hit must not be lifted above knee height. So that all the players are brought into the game, no player may hit the ball back twice running.

To decide which is the winning side, either one counts the number of points scored in a specified time or the game continues until a specified number of points has been reached.

Further drills for the hit — shots at goal — are to be found in the chapter on the goalkeeper (see pp. 154-155, 158-161).

The 'chipped' hit

Whilst in 1980 the chipped hit or lob was only used when under pressure as a means of clearing the ball defensively from one end of the field to the other, already two years later the chip was used by the top teams in the world systematically constructively in the attack. The tendency nowadays goes towards an increased use of the chip in relation to the flick in the same game situation thanks to the possibility:
a) to execute the pass quickly (the 'high' hit can be performed quickly from a 'normal' standing position only opening the face of the stick in the last moment for undercutting the ball which is placed in front of the front foot).
b) to not allow the opponent to anticipate the chip as it is the case with the flicked aerial pass when body positioning and the position of the right hand on the stick allow the opponent to prepare for the pass.
c) to give more speed to the chipped hit, which means that the chip generally reaches the receiver faster.

The chip is especially successful when it is used diagonally, for instance from the right inside position towards the left wing position by-passing several defenders who are no more allowed to use their hands for intercepting the aerial pass.

Special attention should be dedicated to the reception of the chipped hits. In order to avoid the ball bouncing awkwardly, which gives the defender time to recover the ball or at least time to position himself adequately when the ball was controlled by the attacker, the receiver should preferably collect the ball in the air, mainly on the run, which, of course, demands a perfect understanding between the passer and receiver.

The force of the hit

For the ball to be hit properly certain requirements must be met. In the first place the ball must be struck accurately to reach its target. The player must, therefore, master the technique of producing a clean hit both when stationary and when on the run. Apart from the accuracy of the hit, the force with which the ball is hit must correspond to the player's tactical intentions. In order to be able to impart considerable speed to the ball, when shooting at goal or passing, the player should be aware of factors which determine the force of the hit.

The force of the hit depends on the following factors, quite apart from correctness of technique and the quality of the extremely stiff hockey-stick:
1. the player's approach speed.
2. the speed of the downswing.
3. the application of body weight.
4. the hardness of the ball.
5. the approach speed of the ball (for a first time shot).

Let us consider these factors separately:

1. The player's approach speed.

The force with which the ball is struck increases in proportion to the speed at which the player himself approaches the ball for the hit. The impetus gained from the approach increases the power which is applied to the ball. This fact is not sufficiently heeded by many players; otherwise they would no longer take a stationary shot at goal after a stick stopped corner or after a short, slow approach to the ball.

If the marksman wants to strike the ball really hard, he must approach it at top speed. Only in his last stride before the hit must the player's approach be somewhat slowed down to allow him to concentrate on the correct execution of the hit.

2. Speed of the downswing

The further back the stick is taken, the greater is the acceleration which can be given the the stick on its now lengthened path to the ball. Therefore for a hard hit, not only the player's approach speed is of importance but also the extent of the backswing and, with it, the speed at which the stickhead meets the ball.

The acceleration of the stick must be such that it reaches its maximum speed at the moment of impact with the ball. But in order to achieve considerable speed for the stickhead at the moment of impact, after a relatively short backswing, great force and perfect co-ordination are necessary. The greater the degree of development of the resilience of the player's muscles in relation to his body weight, the easier it is to move the arms and the stick quickly. As women are less muscular than men, they are unable to move their arms as quickly and therefore cannot hit as hard as men.

3. Application of body weight

The weight of the body must not be overlooked when hitting the ball hard. Since the tightly gripping hands form a connecting link between the stick and the body, it is impossible for the weight of the stick alone to be effective in producing the force needed for the hit, and inevitably part of the player's body weight (especially the right hip which rotates with the downswing into the direction of the hit) is involved. How much of the player's weight can be brought into play during the hit, depends upon the degree of muscular tension and technique. At the moment of impact, all the muscles involved in the movement of the downswing must be fully tensed, in order to make a really hard hit possible. If, for example, you make a hit with the wrists held slack you will never achieve maximum force, because the firmness of the connecting link between stick and body has been relaxed, with the result that the effect of the body weight is lost. A whippy, yielding stick, too, counteracts the advantages gained by good muscle tension, reducing the force of the hit. (In tennis you can hit harder with a tightly strung racket than you can with a loosely strung one.)

The degree of muscular tension that can be brought to bear at the moment of impact depends on the player's muscle power, thus the stronger individual uses his body weight to greater advantage. Because women cannot produce the same degree of muscular tension in their arms and trunk as men, since their muscles are weaker, the ball does not come off their stick, even when tightly gripped, with the same velocity. This reduced degree of muscular tension is frequently evidenced among women by a visible shaking of the body at the moment of impact between stick and ball.

To sum up, it can be said that a player brought up on a regular programme of power and muscle-resilience training can attain a greater degree of muscular tension at the moment of impact; as a consequence of which, the body weight can be more efficiently applied and so, finally, a harder hit is achieved than is possible with a player who has not yet taken power training into consideration in his training programme.

4. The hardness of the ball

At the moment of impact, the surface of the ball is very slightly dented. Because of its elasticity, the ball immediately afterwards strives to assume its original shape again. The harder the ball is, the greater the effort the ball makes to do this.

A good example of this is the plastic ball, which is much harder than the traditional leather ball, and which rebounds much more rapidly from the stick. Thus it can be hit much harder.

5. *The approach speed of the ball*

Considerable extra force can be imparted to the ball by a first time shot at goal, if the ball is coming as a rebound from the opponent or also as a pass from a team-mate.

The greater the speed of the approaching ball, the greater is the force of the impact between stick and ball and, consequently, the harder the shot becomes; it then also carries a greater element of surprise.

The shot at goal

Every action of the attacking side is directed at getting into the circle and producing a successful shot at the opponent's goal. For your players, especially, the shot at goal is a pleasurable aspect of the game's technique, which they will practise enthusiastically for hours (see Chapter 25 in *'The Advanced Science of Hockey'* — Is our way of teaching children hockey still up-to-date?). The dual between forward and goalkeeper fascinates them. Every young player would like to beat the goalkeeper so they take special delight in trying to lift their shots at goal.

The most suitable places for the shot at goal, however, are its two lower corners, especially the left hand corner which the goalie cannot reach with his stick. Shots at goal along the ground are very dangerous for the goalkeeper, because he needs more time to save with his feet than for saving a high ball with the stick or hand. Therefore shots at goal along the ground are more successful than high ones, when the speed of the ball is taken into consideration, for the low ball.

If the shot at goal does go in the air, however, it is more difficult for the goalie to stop when placed in the upper right hand corner of the goal. This is because the goalie's free hand can be moved more quickly than his right hand which is holding the stick; he would, of course, give away a penalty stroke if he were to raise that above his shoulder.

Before the forward shoots at goal, he should be able to note out of the corner of his eye in a fraction of a second the position, not only of the goalie, but also the position of the backs. If the position of the backs is such that there is no gap at all for the shot or if only a very unfavourable angle is left, then the forward should look for the chance of passing to a better placed team-mate.

Generally speaking the shot at goal should be made as soon as the forward has crossed the edge of the circle. For this reason all forwards must be able to shoot hard and quickly at top speed, even when the right foot is forwards at the moment of shooting (*Fig. 37* page 46).

As the ball can easily rebound from the goalie's pads or even from the goalposts, the forward should always continue towards goal after getting his shot in to take advantage of any chance of scoring that might arise before the nearest defender can intervene. Almost 30% of goals are scored from offensive rebounds. It is not sufficient, though, for only the one player to do this; the other forwards who are in the vicinity of the goal, must also follow up. In order to make this a natural and automatic reaction among the forwards, all practices for shooting at goal (see 'Defensive Technique when making a stop' pages 158-161) should be carried out with a second forward running in with the player shooting at goal and both of them striving to score from the follow-up.

Among advanced players the shot at goal is no longer practised with the player stationary or after dribbling, as it is with the beginners; now it is linked in with other aspects of technique, for example, passing, receiving, beating a man and the dummy. By means of practising, at first with weak but later with more experienced defenders, the shot at goal must be carried out under match conditions (see chapter 10 in *The Advanced Science of Hockey* – 'Scoring goals').

To give the goalie some interest in the competition, the practice in shooting at goal should be a game-like situation with an integrated sequence of actions involved. That is why group practice is to be preferred to practice between individuals. Which team scores the most goals within a specified period of time? Which team is the first to get ten (fifteen) shots on target? Which team achieves the lowest number of shots off target? To obtain maximum success in these contests, the players, in practising shooting at goal against opposition, should try to coordinate the force of the hit with accuracy of direction. The greater the distance from goal, the harder the ball must be hit; even a well aimed shot from the edge of the circle can be easily saved if the ball has only been hit softly because the goalkeeper has sufficient time to adjust his position relative to the speed and direction of the ball.

The goalie will have considerably more difficulty, however, in assessing the speed and direction of the ball, if the opponent does not attempt to control the ball before shooting. The first time shot at goal generally comes so hard and unexpectedly that the goalkeeper scarcely manages to react at all.

If the goalie, in order to narrow the angle, runs out to meet the opponent attempting to get his shot in, the forward should beat him preferably on his reverse stick side or simply put the ball past him.

During the course of the game countless attacks are mounted. Less than 6% generally culminate with a favourable opportunity for a shot at goal. So as not to squander too many chances for a successful shot at goal, the forwards must use opportunities with especial concentration, determination and prudence. Just as important as concentration at the moment of shooting, determination and prudence when aiming, is self-confidence. Those players who trust their shooting power are generally the best. A lack of self-confidence can only have a detrimental effect on the difficult skill of shooting at goal when at top speed, as well as on all other difficult techniques.

The penalty corner

One notices time and time again that moderate teams with excellent goalkeepers and a reliable marksman at penalty corners can beat technically superior teams.

The reason for the surprising defeat of the favourites is generally to be found in their poor technique when taking penalty corners. One frequently sees up to a dozen corners wasted because of lack of concentration, careless positioning and too much improvisation in execution. It must be added that the penalty corner is grossly neglected in training especially by club teams. 'Everything will work out all right in the match' — or so it is hoped. Nowadays however, the importance of extensive practice in taking short corners is proved by the fact that in matches, goals from open play become rarer.

Three reliable players are needed when taking a direct penalty corner and one mistake by any of them results in failure. For a penalty corner to be taken successfully, certain basic aspects of hockey technique must be mastered.
1. The ball must be hit, or better, pushed without any preparation at moderate speed, accurately from the goal line to the edge of the circle. A push is preferable to a hit as the waiting defenders have great difficulty in estimating the exact moment that the ball is coming out because of the absence of a backswing.
2. The ball must be stopped cleanly and motionless with the stick (see pages 37-38).
3. It must be hit when completely stationary as hard as possible at the goal or passed as set move to one of the other team mates available.
4. After a shot on goal, the seven players involved in the penalty corner should go for the offensive rebound (see *Fig. 44b*) covering a zone which has been contributed to them before the match.

The simplicity of these four requirements could give rise to the false conclusion that penalty corners should generally lead to goals. But the opposition, for their part, are doing everything to prevent a penalty corner from being carried out successfully. It is not that simple to beat a good goalkeeper who is supported by five team-mates on the goal-line or out on the way towards the striker, with one shot or some prestudied passes, and the prospects for the goalkeeper (and therefore for the team in defence) of winning this duel are generally fairly good.

The 25 most important hints for a successful penalty corner push-out, stop and hit-in

The push-out:
1. The push should be preferred to the hit-out because of
   — more accuracy
   — the possibility to hide the precise moment of playing the ball and to surprise the opponents running out
   — the facilities to vary the rhythm between placing and playing the ball
   — less possibilities for the opponents to anticipate it.
2. The ball should be passed with the initial part of the curve. The handle of the stick is level with the knees and the feet are separated more than shoulder wide.
3. A transfer of the weight of the body from the right towards the left foot should not be executed in order to avoid the opponents anticipating the push. Without moving the trunk, the push should be carried out explosively, using the strength of the forearms and wrists.
4. After the push, the curve should be kept low, as close to the ground as possible.
5. The push should have maximum speed to allow sufficient time for stopping and hitting in.

The stop
1. The place of stopping the ball depends on the behaviour of the goalkeeper and the speed of the first player running out.
2. Always approach the ball with the same number of steps starting always from the same low starting position with the right foot advanced and the legs sufficiently bent (like the 'take-off' for a long distance race).
3. A low position of the body permits a good observation of the oncoming ball. Observe its direction and its possible bounce carefully until the ball touches your stick which was laid down horizontally on the ground with the curve pointing towards the left with its point into the ground. (*Fig. 30*)
4. Keep your arms relaxed with both hands employing a loose grip on the stick.
5. When stopping, both arms are almost fully stretched to ensure that the ball is sufficiently apart from the body in front of the right foot.
6. The stick has to be placed in a right angle to the direction of the oncoming ball.

7. Absorb the chock between the oncoming ball and stick through very slightly bent arms, loose grip and a special preparation of the label of the stick that is the part with which the ball has to be stopped.
8. Decide in a split second about a possible change in your method of stopping when the ball bounces or lacks on accuracy in its direction.
9. After having stopped the ball completely stationary, both hands move the stick as fast as possible towards the right hip.
10. After moving the stick away the same player should change the position of his hands on the stick and prepare (with the right hand in its centre) for a possible quick rebound or other intervention.

The hit-in
1. Decide in advance the point in front of the goal from which the ball has to be hit.
2. The weight of the curve of the stick of the striker should be superior to that of all other players. Also give importance to the stiffness of the handle.
3. When moving to the oncoming ball, the timing and the rhythm in executing always the same number of steps are important.
4. The techniques of striking the ball are different to those of the normal hits used in the field. The technique depends on the behaviour of the opposing goalkeeper.
5. The time between stopping and hitting should be kept as short as possible.
6. Trying to hit the ball with maximum strength and maximum efforts may result in poor co-ordination and therefore in a poor direction of the shot.
7. Lifting the head immediately after impact results often in a possible poor shot.
8. The strong and weak points of the opposing goalkeeper and his defenders on the goalline determine the direction of the striker's shot or pass.
9. Once the ball is on the way towards the opposing goal, the striker has to anticipate to take a rebound.
10. Train the hit-in under pressure as often as possible in order to gain accuracy, perfection and confidence.

The first requirement in the defence of a penalty corner is to ensure that the line of vision for the goalkeeper and the two defenders standing on the goal-line is never obscured; therefore, the fastest player should run out of the left side of the goal towards the corner-striker with the stick held in the right hand only. A second and third player, placed outside the goal beside each

Fig. 44a. Penalty corner for India taken from the right side of the goal against Pakistan, 1983, in Karachi

Fig. 44b. Penalty corner for Germany taken from the left side of the goal against New Zealand, 1983, in Karachi

post generally move out three or four metres, so as to take any balls on the rebound and to clear them from the danger zone with a push.

In support of the three players in the goalmouth and the three leaving the goal-line in the moment of hit out*, at least two of the forwards should run back from behind the centre-line to the circle as quickly as they are allowed to by the rules to help in the defence.

If the opposing team master the penalty corner to a high extent (which actually happens very often), the defence should be organised somewhat differently. In this case the goalkeeper sprints out as far as possible towards the stopper, so as to narrow the angle of the impending shot at goal. The closer he is at the moment the shot or flick is taken, the greater his chances are of making a save, whilst standing up (saving a flick) or whilst laying parallel to the goalline on the ground (saving a hit). In order to prevent the striker passing to his left or right to another player, the goalkeeper is accompanied out by a defender on both his left and right hand side, who are also covered in case of failure (*Fig. 45*). A fourth player runs first to the edge of the circle or acts as the sweeper behind the first defensive line and the fifth and sixth players stand with their heels touching the goalline in either side of the goal.

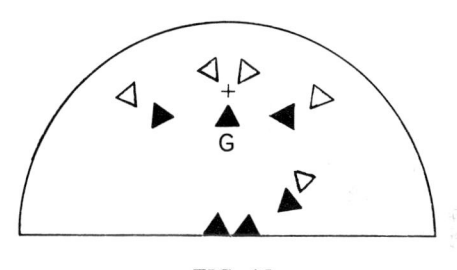

FIG. 45

Disguising the direction of the hit

To hit the ball accurately and in the direction intended, the player must, of course, first master the technique of hitting. However, if the ball is not hit precisely with the correct section of the blade, then spin is imparted to it. Balls with spin can therefore occur partly quite unintentionally because of mistakes in technique. But situations quite often occur during the game in which the use of such a technique can well be advisable for tactical reasons.

---

* for more detailed information concerning the penalty corner in attack and defence refer to '*The Advanced Science of Hockey*' 2nd ed.

Balls which are intentionally sliced and which hence give a misleading idea as to the direction the hit finally takes, can only be produced by players of the highest technical and tactical ability.

Before the player learns to disguise the direction of his hitting, he should first of all master two simpler methods for deceiving his opponent. The first is to avoid looking in the direction along which the ball is to be hit. The second method is to take up a misleading stance in order to deceive the opponent and not until the backswing is the left shoulder brought round into the different direction along which the ball will actually travel. For instance the centre half, standing with the ball on the 22.90m line, wants to send a free hit to his centre forward. In order to deceive his opponents he places himself so that his left shoulder points towards his outside left or outside right. By means of a quick turn during the backswing, he brings his left shoulder round into the direction of the centre forward who finally receives the ball.

For learning how to disguise the direction of a hit to the left, the player must take up the side-on position to the ball. From this position the ball can be hit without great difficulty in such a way that the opponent cannot anticipate its direction. By maintaining the player's normal position *vis-a-vis* the ball, it becomes possible to alter the direction of the hit at the very last moment. For a clearer understanding of this, an example must be added. If, while taking a free hit, the centre half stands side-on, pointing in the direction of the outside right, the opposition will try to interpret his intentions from the position he adopts and they will concentrate therefore on the direction that they anticipate the ball will take.

The centre half has noticed out of the corner of his eye where his opponents have placed themselves in anticipation of the hit. As already mentioned, he first of all swings back the stick as usual for a normal hit and starts to bring the stick down towards the ball in the line along which his left shoulder is also pointing. Only at the very last second, directly before the stickhead meets the ball, the player, using his right wrist, turns the stick slightly towards the left ('top-spin') and, with the stickface slightly tilted towards the left, the hit is carried out in a different direction, i.e. towards the centre forward. To make this hit to the left easier, the ball should lie further than is otherwise normal in front of the left foot.

If, in order to disguise the direction of a hit made to the left, the ball has to be struck to the right of centre, then conversely if force is applied to the ball to the left of centre, a hit to the right will result. And the further the ball is hit to the side, the more it will deviate sideways from the anticipated straight line.

When the intention is to disguise the direction of a hit made to the right,

as in this latter example, the player must stand far enough away from the ball for the stick to swing freely in its arc between the right leg and the ball. It can then strike the ball to the left of centre on that face of the ball which is pointing directly towards the right foot. The disguised hit to the right varies in many respects from the normal hit, the most important of which are:
1. The position of the stick face relative to the ball is, at the moment of impact, quite different. In this case the ball is not hit centrally but to the side of its mid-point.
2. Striking the ball is rendered more difficult because the preparation phase does not correspond to the distance, power and speed of the main action of the hit.
3. The ball is sliced rather than hit. To achieve this, the area of the stick face is made to slide round the ball by giving it a slight turn to the left with the right wrist, so that the palm of the right hand is pointing slightly upwards. Because of this slice the ball will travel more slowly than one which has been hit dead centre even though the speed of the hit is the same. The reason for this is that the full weight of the body cannot be transmitted to the ball. It is also much more difficult to calculate accurately the force of a disguised hit.
4. One of the most important features of the disguised hit to the right is the change in the direction of the hit at the very last moment.

One sees the disguised hit to the left more frequently in a match than the disguised hit to the right. One sees the latter used especially when a free hit is taken immediately outside the opponent's circle. The centre half, for example, positions himself in such a way that his left shoulder is pointing towards his inside left. Neither his pick-up nor the actual downswing give any indication at first of any different direction for the free hit to take than to his inside forward.

Only at the very end of the downswing, without any alteration in the player's stance, is the ball heavily sliced by means of the change in the position of the stickhead and a change in position of the point of impact, so that the ball skews off abruptly into an open space in the direction of the centre forward.

Practice drills to encourage the use of the disguised hit and to help improve its technical application under match conditions:

1. Two teams each with three players line up opposite each other 22.90m apart, across the width of the normal hockey pitch. A third team with two or three players takes up its position in the middle between the other two sides (*Fig. 46*). The two outside teams now attempt to pass the ball to each

other through the gaps in the middle team, while the players in the middle strive to prevent them. The players in the outside teams are allowed to pass the ball among themselves (for a maximum of three times) so as to find a favourable opportunity for a pass through the middle.

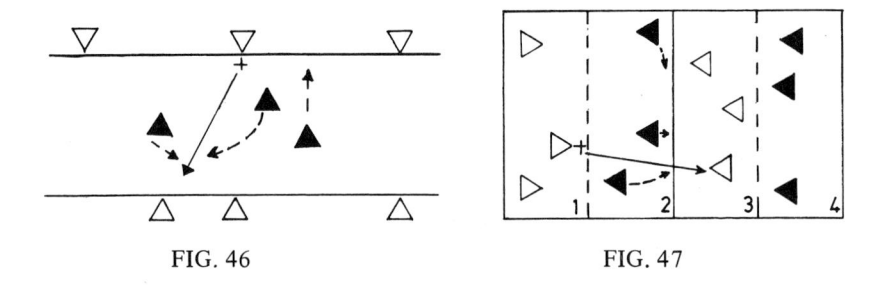

FIG. 46

FIG. 47

2. Two teams with six players in each are divided up into two equal groups. The groups take up their positions on the pitch as shown in *Fig. 47*. Team A occupies areas 1 and 3, Team B areas 2 and 4. The players attempt to get the ball through to the other group of their own players, so that the players in the middle cannot intercept the pass which must not rise above knee level. This practice takes place on a normal hockey pitch. The winning team is the one to achieve the most passes within a certain time.
3. 'Spy in the Camp': Two teams each with three players are separated from each other by a neutral strip 10-20m wide. Each group sends one man (the fourth player) into the enemy camp. His own team-mates attempt to pass the ball to this spy. If they succeed, the player who passed the ball changes over into the enemy camp as a second spy. Which side will get all its men as spies into the opponents' camp first?
4. 'Disguise the Ball': Four against four on the whole field across the goal-line. The aim is to hit the goal across the opposing goal line.

6 The Flick

The flick, which in earlier days was very rarely seen, is today, because of the introduction of the penalty stroke (1961), the use of close marking (1965) and the importance of indoor hockey for a field hockey player, part and parcel of the modern game. Although as early as 1928, the Indians, in their first Olympic victory in Amsterdam, demonstrated that the flick could be used both as a means of passing and also of shooting at goal, it was more than thirty years before its full significance and possibilities were properly recognised. Even in the middle sixties flicking the ball in mid-field over the head of an opponent to a team-mate moving into the open spaces was avoided because of possible danger; it would also have been taken as proof that the player lacked mastery over other techniques. It was only dangerous in those days, because very few players understood how to flick the ball with control and accuracy. Gradually, however, especially among active players, the opinion began to prevail that a ball flicked at goal, and especially a high aerial flick carried out at the correct moment with full regard for the state of the play, demands not only a high degree of technical ability but also a certain degree of mental application. It is just this ability to weigh up the right moment to

Fig. 48

produce a high flick with the correct direction, height and speed over the opponents, who mark very tightly, to a fast player running into an open space which demands a mental agility and an optical-physical assessment that not all players possess.

How to teach the flick

A pre-requisite for learning the flick is complete mastery of the pushed pass.

The basic position, as well as the grip on the stick, is the same in flicking as in pushing. However, as the ball should leave the ground when flicked, the stickhead has to be placed not only behind but also somewhat beneath the ball. That is only possible, however, if the ball is placed a little to the left in front of the left foot and if the upper part of the stick is inclined backwards to the right pointing into the right knee. As with putting the shot, the weight of the body is then placed emphatically onto the bent right leg, in the side-on position, so that the player can see 'under' the ball.

To perform a flick over a longer distance it is generally necessary to use body weight. The player should take up a position a full stride from the ball. As he reaches forward to make contact with the ball he should transfer his weight from his right to his left foot. The flick action of the wrists and forearms should be carried out at the same time as the stick gets in contact with the ball and the player finishes by transferring this weight towards the front foot. This will add considerably to the shot. Whilst the right wrist operates along the line which the ball is being sent, the left wrist, on the other hand, moves the stick in the opposite direction and levers the curve of the stick upwards.

Today top-class players often use another, more difficult method of flicking the ball. Without adjusting the body, with both hands close together at the top of the stick they manage to flick the ball over long distances thanks to their strength in the forearms. Deceiving (through body position and hand positions) their intention until the very last second, the opponent very often has no chance to react to this surprising aerial pass.

Methodical series of drills : from flicking the ball at rest, with the player stationary, to flicking a moving ball when on the run:

1. *Flicking against a wall.*
   To make the task more difficult, a circle can be drawn, into which the ball has to be flicked, or a line some three or four metres high can be drawn, over which the ball has to be flicked. The distance from the wall is increased in proportion to the increasing mastery of the shot.

2. Flicking with a partner, combined with stopping the high ball. The distance should be between 6-22.90m.
3. Three players, standing eight to twenty metres from each other along a line, flick the ball to each other. In this practice the ball must always be flicked over the head of the player in the middle to the other outside player. After each flick the player changes with the man in the middle.
4. *'Chase the Ball'.*
   The aim of this flicking competition, played across the width of a hockey pitch between the centre and 22.90m line, is to flick the ball over the line at the far end (the side-line of the normal pitch). The game begins with a flick 5m in from one side-line. Where the ball is stopped dead by the opponents, the next flick can be carried out in the other direction.
5. *Practice for the penalty stroke.*
   In order to practise the penalty stroke, the ball is flicked into the left and right hand corners of the goal, almost along the ground as well as into the top of the goal (on the stick side and on the free hand). Advanced players should also practise disguising the direction of the flick.
6. Flicking the stationary ball while running, the left leg being placed forward at the moment of the flick.
7. Flicking a stationary ball at the goal while running with the right leg being placed forward at the moment of flicking (*Fig. 49*). With this

Fig. 49. Top class players like Errman of India must be able to master the flick even when the right foot is forward

Fig. 50. The reverse stick flick or the reverse stick slap shot should be mastered by all forwards against goalkeepers when they fling themselves close to the goal in a left inside position

    difficult skill, attention must be paid to see that the upper part of the body is inclined well forward and is over the ball.

8.
a) After dribbling a short distance the ball should be stopped on the 22.90m line with the reverse stick and flicked as quickly as possible to another player behind the centre line, who then flicks the ball back over a third player so that this last cannot reach the ball. This should be done successfully ten times.
b) With increasing sureness in flicking, the ball need no longer be stopped but can be flicked while still rolling.
9. After beating a passive defender 10m away from goal on his reverse stick side, the ball, still rolling, is then flicked directly at goal without being stopped. The left foot at the moment of flicking should be forward.
10. After beating a passive defender 10m away from goal on his forehand side, the player should flick the still rolling ball with reverse stick at goal. The practice should be carried out with the left foot and later the right foot forward at the moment of flicking.

Use in the game*

The uses of the flick in the game of hockey are many and varied. The placing of the ball is very important as the player using a flick may be penalised for dangerous play.

A player in possession of the ball approaching an opponent with an open space behind him (as happens frequently in the wing positions) can quickly flick the ball over his opponent's stick (especially when laid down horizontally on the ground) and continue his attack. The skill of raising the ball very slightly above the surface (flipping it up), carried out by a quick wrist action, must be disguised up until the last moment otherwise the opponent will anticipate the attacking move. Since it is not necessary to change the position of the body or feet to make such a gentle flick above the outstretched stick it is easy to disguise it. Care should be taken that when dribbling the ball the stickhead is advanced in relation to the position of the wrists!

More often a flick is used as a pass when there is one or more players between the passer and the receiver. Instead of trying to beat the player and then pass the ball, which means a big risk and which also takes time and allows more opposing players to cover the play, the attacker can use a more or less long and high flick. This can be especially effective when used as a diagonal pass from the centre half to one wing, a space which the sweeper generally cannot cover. When raised high above the heads of all defenders it will cause no danger and is very difficult to intercept. The ball should be placed to land in space ahead of the receiver and the onus is on him to make his run to collect the ball immediately before it bounces on the artificial turf or after it has hit the natural grass. In order to ensure success with this pass, a perfect mutual understanding between passer and receiver is necessary.

The flick is probably most often used as a shot at goal. Because of the fact that the stick does not have to be raised from the ball to execute the shot, the flick is a quick and most unexpected stroke. For these reasons it is very difficult for the goalkeeper to anticipate the direction in which the ball may go, especially when the flick is well disguised.

Sometimes a flick is the only choice open to a player because he finds himself in a position when a hit would be impossible (*Fig. 51a*). If for instance the ball is loose in the circle and there is a race to get there, the flick or push is the better shot for the forward to use. A hit takes too much time because the player has to get his feet almost level with the ball and be properly balanced. A player who finds himself very close to the goalline, a few metres

---

*see also Barbara Smith in 'Lifting the Ball', paper for the FIH Coaching Course in Mexico City, 1980.

to the left of the goal (from the attacker's point of view) and under pressure will not have any chance to turn around for a pass or to aim a drive at the goal. Even a reverse stick shot will be difficult to pull off from that angle (*Fig. 51b*). However, a flick directed towards the right corner of the goal will be possible to execute. When running towards the goal with the ball in front of him, the attacker can flick the ball quickly at the goal by reaching out and flicking using only his forearms (*Fig. 50*).

Fig. 51a. Charlesworth (Australia) ready to flick the ball past the German goalkeeper Ludwiczak.

Fig. 51b. P. Litjens tries to score with reverse stick against Aslam from Pakistan

For the penalty stroke a flick is almost invariably used. When executed very well the goalkeeper has virtually no chance of saving a penalty stroke. Experienced players master lifting the ball whilst disguising the direction of the shot by a sudden movement of the wrists without losing any speed. However, beginners or less experienced players should not lose speed, as it is basically the velocity of the ball that beats the goalkeeper. Those learning to take penalty shots must concentrate first on flicking hard and low.

7 Beating an Opponent

In a match every player should do his utmost to work for the benefit of his side and to be careful not to do anything which might detract from this. While holding on to the ball unnecessarily (especially attempting to get round an opponent) hinders rather than helps the side's interests, a quick and well-conceived pass to a team-mate is usually more profitable. However, on occasions, it is necessary to hold on to the ball to beat an opponent as situations frequently arise, especially for those players who spearhead the attack, in which no team-mate is available for a pass.

There are various methods of getting round an opponent. If a player always uses the same one, then the person marking him will soon find the defensive answer. Success in beating opponents depends, therefore, not only on correct technical execution but also on variation. Thus a good player is required not only to know of the various methods of beating an opponent but also to have complete mastery over them.

Fig. 52. Mahendran of Malaysia beats a New Zealand defender in the Third World Cup opening match in Kuala Lumpur in 1975

1. **Pushing the ball past the opponent**

   The simplest method of beating an opponent is to push the ball past him (between his left hand and left foot on his reverse stick side, and on his forehand or flipping the ball, over the outstretched stick or by pushing it between his legs) and then, after a short sprint round to his opponent's left, to take possession of the ball again (*Fig. 52*). Pursuit, after an attempt to tackle has failed, generally costs the defender so much time that the forward is already out of range.

   This method of beating an opponent is especially profitable when the pace of the game is hot. But it is important to see that the time elapsing between the ball being pushed forward and being brought back into possession again is kept as short as possible. Pushing the ball past the opponent must take place neither too early nor too late. The choice of the exact moment is generally the deciding factor for the success of the attempt. If at all possible the dribbler should look up from the ball and then push it past the opponent when the latter begins his attempt to tackle.

   If the player pushes the ball forward too soon, the defender realises what his real intentions are and will almost certainly halt the attack. But if the forward pushes the ball round the opponent too late, that is to say, within the immediate range of the defender without observing the stick movements of the defender – which happens very frequently – he runs the risk that the ball will hit the defender's stick and be lost.

Methodical series of drills for learning how to beat an opponent by pushing the ball past him.

a) Two groups of players line up opposite each other about seventy-five metres apart. Between each group six flags or cones are placed at twelve metre intervals (*Fig. 53*). The players pass the ball to the right of each flag along the ground or lifting it slightly over an imaginary opponent's stick and then run round it to the left.

   Having completed the six attempts at rounding the flags, the player passes the ball over to the next player in the other group.

   On artificial grass turfs and levelled natural grass fields the attacking player should dribble always with the ball in continuous contact with the

FIG. 53

curve (the stick is slightly inclined backwards with the hands never above the curve) which enables him to flip the ball past the defender in the moment of his defensive action.

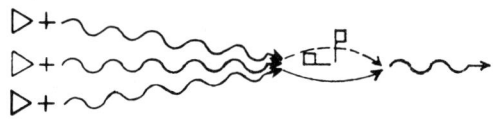

FIG. 54

In order to achieve a higher percentage of success in beating an opponent, the attacker should approach the defender by driving diagonally across him.
b) A mistake commonly seen in the course of this method of rounding an opponent is that the ball is brought too close to the defender. In this case the defender can win the ball without any great difficulty, before any attempt to round him can be made, simply by use of the defender's reach. As an indication, therefore, of a player's reach, a second flag is laid on the ground in front of every upright flag (the imaginary defender), so that it points towards the player (*Fig. 54*). The dribbler now has to push the ball past the upright flag before reaching the one on the ground.
c) Six players, who form passive opposition, take the place of the six standing flags. However, the flags lying on the ground in front of the defenders indicating their reach, remain.
d) This time the flags on the ground are also removed. The players should now indicate the extent of their reach by lunging forward and going through the motions of tackling, so as to give the dribbler an idea of the exact spot at which the ball has to be flipped past the defender.
e) The players now provide active opposition but are not allowed to retreat in defence (see 'Tackling in retreat p. 132). In this practice, the attackers should learn to keep a careful eye on the defender. At the precise moment that the defender attempts a frontal block tackle, the dribbler must push or flip the ball past him. After this 'stratagem' the dribbler runs round the defender with a short burst of speed and regains possession of the ball behind the defender. The simple method of rounding an opponent by pushing or flipping the ball past his left-hand side, or even through his legs or over his outstretched stick on his right side should be used especially when the defender commits the tactical error of moving in to tackle the attacking forward.
f) The forward runs up to the standing defender and stops the ball suddenly on the reverse stick about 3m outside the defender's reach. At this, the latter generally lunges well forward, which the attacker was anticipating

and for which he is therefore fully prepared. The moment the defender begins his tackle, the attacker pushes the ball past him or lifts it slightly over his stick.

g) Playing the ball through the defender's legs is generally not as successful as playing the ball round the defender's body, because the defender can, and frequently does, stop the ball illegally by quickly closing his legs. If, however, the player feints before then pushing it through the defender's legs, his chances of success will be much improved. An example: after dribbling on the right the forward takes the ball in front of his body, just before making the attempt to round his opponent. Whilst still outside the reach of the defender, the ball is suddenly pulled about a metre to the left of the player's direct path and then, immediately afterwards, it is passed with the reverse stick, diagonally to the right, through the legs of the defender, which are now wide open (*Fig. 55*). The success of the attacker's deception derives from the ball being pulled sideways to the left which then causes the defender to alter his basic position. This change in stance generally produces a movement to the right, thus forcing the legs further apart than usual. The moment the defender follows the sideways movement of the forward by moving his legs further apart, it is now a simple matter to place a reverse stick pass through his legs.

FIG. 55

2. **Beating an opponent by means of a sudden change of direction and speed**

Another method of beating an opponent is to break away suddenly from the straight line along which the forward is running and to begin to dribble the ball in a wide arc to the left or right of the defender. Whilst dribbling, the forward watches carefully to see whether the defender is following or not. If the defender does not, the forward should dribble straight past the defender with an explosive burst of pace into the open space. If the defender sets off in pursuit of the attacker, however, the latter, after his first, misleading movement, suddenly carries out, quite unexpectedly, a second intentional movement in the opposite direction (*Figs. 56 and 57*).

Only after a certain time lapse can the defender manage to follow this second movement (*Fig. 59c*) for which the attacker was fully prepared but not the defender. In fact, by the time the defender has been able to halt his initial movement and follow the forward, who has dodged off

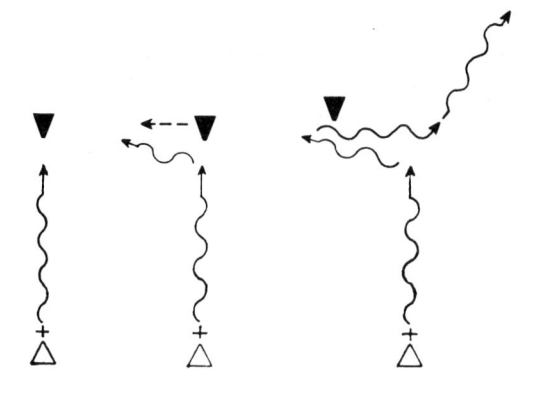

Fig. 56. Beating an opponent on his reverse stick by a sudden change in direction

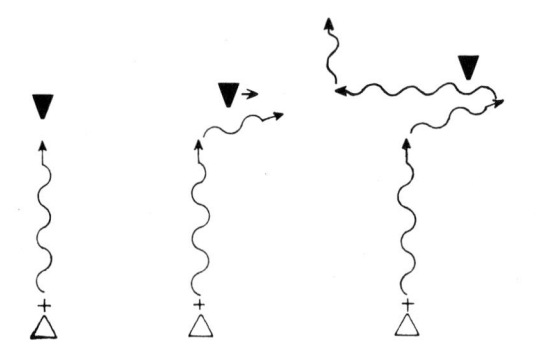

Fig. 57. Beating an opponent on his front stick by a sudden change in direction

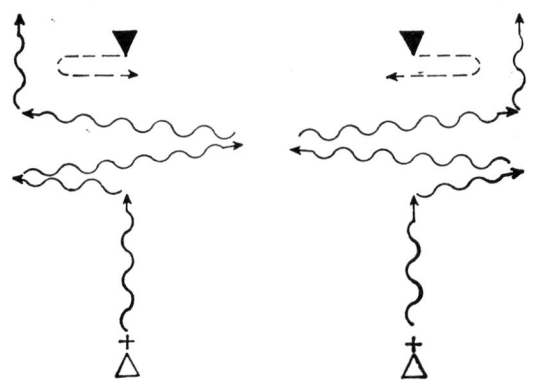

Fig. 58. Beating an opponent on his left- or right-hand side changing the direction twice

in the opposite direction, the forward has generally been able to get completely free to one side or the other. If unexpectedly the defender is not shaken off by this sudden change of direction, the attacker, whilst still out of the defender's reach, has to try dodging back again along the direction of the very first movement (*Fig. 58*).

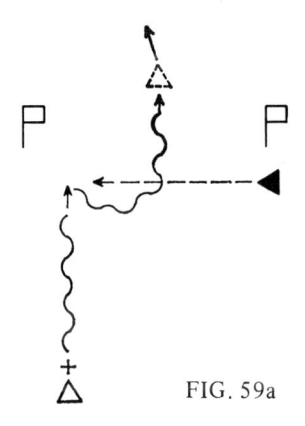

FIG. 59a

A further slight variation for beating an opponent by means of a sudden change of direction is best illustrated by the following situation: the centre forward has broken past the centre half and is now bearing down alone on the opponent's circle. Since he is on the point of entering the circle and getting in a shot at goal, the left back, having rapidly summed up the situation, decides to tackle the centre forward and so runs across to meet him (*Fig. 59a*). A good centre forward will notice this, however, and, just before the back reaches him, will change direction. Keeping outside the back's reach, he dodges to the right, dribbling the ball for a few paces in the direction from which the back has just come, thus causing the back to run past him and allowing himself to dribble on to goal. This method of getting round the opposition demands considerable practice. But when carried out carefully and with concentration, its success will delight the forward and, above all, will increase his self-confidence.

Methodical series of drills for beating an opponent by a sudden change of direction and speed:

a) Test

Without touching the two 3m lines which form a right angle, the player dribbles the ball alternatively up and down for twenty or thirty seconds. After reaching the top (end) of each 3m line, the player suddenly stops on his outside foot, turns around (facing always inside) and simultaneously pushes the ball, without first stopping it, almost back to the base of the right angle, using the reverse stick pass when turning to the right hand side and using the forehand when switching to the left.

When changing the direction of the dribble at the end of the 3m line, the point of gravity should be very close to the ground with femur and tibia forming a right angle. Immediately after having touched the ball at the turning point only *once* the player is changing direction and accelerates to reach the starting point (base) as fast as possible.

For each 3m dribble the player receives one point. How many points can the player achieve by practising this exercise for thirty seconds?

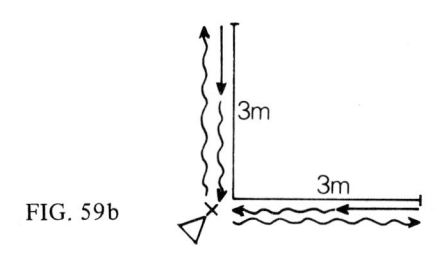

FIG. 59b

b) *Double V*

Each player dribbles his ball diagonally towards the left (or right) and changes suddenly the direction of his dribble, playing the ball slightly backwards to get out of the imagined opponent's reach, describing always a V.

Initially each player decides when and where the change of direction and speed of his dribbling takes place. Later on the trainer calls or signals for the sudden change of direction and speed.

c) *Beating a disadvantaged opponent*

A defender placed in front of the left (right) post of a 12m wide goal should prevent an attacker placed 9m in front of the right (left) goal post from dribbling across the goal line. When the attacker starts his individual attack, the defender is allowed to move towards the centre of the goal with the aim of narrowing the gap in the goal before the attacker suddenly changes the direction of his attack and penetrates on the opposite side where the free space exists (*Fig. 59c*).

If the sudden change of direction and speed by the attacker has not created sufficient space to beat the defender, the attacker has to change direction a second time, without coming within reach of the defender's stick.

Fig. 59c. Surrindher (India) a second before controlling the ball again on the front stick after having changed suddenly the direction of his individual attack. Observe the position of the English defender and the high position of the right hand on the stick of the attacker.

During his dribbling, the attacker has to look up in order to observe the defender's actions. If the defender does not close down the gap in the goal, the attacker should continue his straight dribble until he crosses the goal line with the ball under control and the defender behind him.

Beating an opponent is easier to carry out when the opponent is still running towards the attacker. He should make the opponent move in case he meets him in a stationary position.

Variation: The distance to the unoccupied post is the same for the defender and attacker (*Fig. 59a*).

Variation: Instead of being placed close to the left (right) goal post, the defender now stands 9m in front of it, level with the attacker to whom he passes the ball. On receiving the ball, the attacker starts his individual attack into the open goal, while the defender runs back diagonally to prevent the attacker from scoring.

Variation: The centre-forward stands with the ball on the 22.90m line and the left back, without a ball, off to the forward's right on the edge of the circle. While the centre forward should follow the quickest path to get into the circle, the left back sprints towards him to prevent him from getting in his shot at goal (*Fig. 59*). By means of a sudden change in direction to take him along the line which the back is following to tackle him, the centre forward lets the left back pass by on his left and thus gains time for his shot at goal.

But when the back is so slow that he is unable to reach the forward, who has started off on the coach's signal at the same moment, the forward should run straight on and shoot at goal without bothering to try and get round the back first.

Because of the risk of injury when the defender starts from the other side of the circle (the defender in this case trying to prevent the centre forward's shot at goal with a reverse-stick tackle), the forward should only shoot at goal when he has first rounded the back.

Variation: The right or left back makes a bad clearance and passes straight to the opposing centre forward; after passing the ball, he tries to prevent the centre forward from shooting by sprinting back to the circle.

3. **Beating the opponent to the right and left**

The favourite and most common way of beating an opponent is to pull the ball suddenly out of his reach to the left or right. Whereas up to 1978 players on the right hand side of the field preferred to go round their opponents on the right, most players, whose positions were on the left hand side of the field, preferred to beat their opponents on the left. After the defenders – I am thinking here especially of left backs and left halves – have profited from this observation, attackers were told to give up their habit of preferring to beat their opponent on the same side and tried to do the reverse, which gave them a decided advantage over the defender. An attacker trying to be as successful as possible at beating a defender, should be equally good therefore at beating him on either side and, in the match itself, should take care to vary the methods.

Methodical series of drills for beating an opponent to the right (Fig. 60):

a) The easiest and most natural way to learn how to beat an opponent to the right is, when with the 'Indian way' of dribbling the player suddenly pushes the ball in a right angle three or four metres further away towards

Fig. 60. Carlos Roca (Spain) on the way to beat the New Zealand defender on his reverse stick

the right, using the reverse stick. Together with this reverse stick pass, the player pushes himself off the left foot towards the right for recovering possession of the ball as early as possible keeping it beside the right foot out of the reach of the opponent.
b) Six metres in front of the player practising stands a flag representing the imaginary defender. During the approach to the flag, the ball is dribbled on the front stick. Just before reaching the flag, however, it is brought across the body towards the left side of the imaginary opponent, and then suddenly played diagonally off to the right with the reverse stick. At the same moment that the ball is pulled quickly three metres to the right.
c) Two players, each with a ball, stand opposite each other about twelve metres apart. Between them is a flag which they must both approach first in a straight line. Just before reaching the flag they curve out (in order to move the defender in a match) and then suddenly pull the ball back towards the right out of reach of the outbalanced defender. After beating it, they then dribble, protecting the ball on their right side of the body (the stick may be gripped in this moment with the right hand on the top only – see *Fig. 1b*) to their opposite number's starting position and from here, they begin a new attempt at beating the flag at the same

moment that their partner sets off. The simultaneous beating of the flag has a specific purpose; it forces the players to look up from the ball and keep an eye on their partner.

As an indication of the defender's reach, two flags are placed on the ground, in front of the upright flag, in the path of both players. These flags will force the two players to pull the ball to the side at the right moment, and sufficiently wide (3m).

d) Beating an opponent on the right hand side can be made more automatic by playing round flags lined up at 12m intervals (*Fig. 61*). The second player begins when the man in front of him has beaten the second flag.

FIG. 61

e) When the skill of beating an opponent on the right hand side has been sufficiently practised by means of these four preparatory exercises, passive opposition is then introduced. The player acting as defender is only allowed to lunge forwards (but not to the side). In order to ensure that the defence does in fact remain passive, the defender's right heel must remain in constant contact with the flag behind him. After a few attempts at beating his opponent, the attacker will soon work out

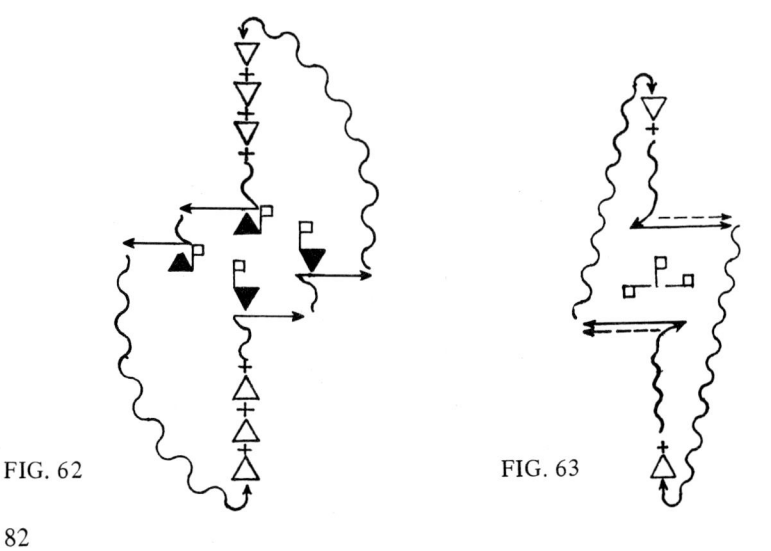

FIG. 62

FIG. 63

that he can always beat the 'anchored' defender when he begins his attempt at the correct moment and remains out of his opponent's reach. At this stage the attacker's attention should be drawn to the necessity for a high approach speed and change of speed when rounding an opponent.

f) As in c) above but with passive defenders who follow the first deceiving move of the attacker towards the opposite side before getting beaten in their reverse stick side.

g) Four defenders form a square (*Fig. 62*). Their sphere of action is again limited in that their right heel must always be touching the flag behind them when they lunge forward. The six attackers continue beating the four passive defenders for two minutes, after which the coach changes the defenders and attackers round.

h) Beating an active defender, placed in front of the circle, on his reverse stick side and scoring against a goal-keeper.

Methodical series of drills for beating an opponent to the left:

a) When dribbling the ball alternately with the front stick and reverse, the player pushes the ball once with his front stick square to the left side (about 3-4m), and collects it there before carrying on to dribble. Special attention must be paid to see that the ball is played left at right angles, i.e. completely square, to the dribbler's normal direction. If this is not heeded and if the ball is played diagonally forwards into the reach of the defender then he will have no difficulty in a match in taking the ball away from the attacker. At exactly the same moment that the ball is pulled sharply sideways, the player pushes off powerfully with his right leg towards the left. After two or three paces towards the left the ball is stopped on the reverse stick and dribbled on again.

b) Six metres in front of the players stands a flag which has to be beaten to the left. On the way to the flag the ball is dribbled to the right of the body; just before reaching the flag, it is brought across the body, midway between the feet, and then in order to deceive the opponent, is moved in a slight curve towards the right and finally pulled very suddenly so that it is absolutely square to the left.

c) Between two players practising is a flag which must be beaten by both of them simultaneously (*Fig. 63*).

In this it is not always necessary, as in a) above, for the ball to be stopped first with the reverse stick after having pulled it sideways to the left. It can also be placed directly onto the right hand side of the body with the reverse stick without having been stopped (Fig. 64).

Fig. 64. Govinder (India) beats Maanzoor sen. (Pakistan) who tries to gain possession of the ball with a jab to the left

d) Four flags (at 12m intervals) must be beaten on the left one after another. Four attempts to beat the flags on the first run are followed by a further four attempts to beat the flags on a return run. This practice can also be carried out in the form of a slalom relay.
e) Getting round the front stick of one of several defenders indicated by flags, is now followed by attempts to get round the front stick of a passive defender, whose right heel must not leave the flag behind him as he attempts to tackle. In the course of this practice the attacker must learn not only to look at the ball but also especially at the defender's stick. At the very moment that the defender starts to make his tackle, the attacker must whip the ball square to the left, pick it up with the reverse stick and then immediately place it back again into the normal dribbling position on the right hand side of the body.
f) Beating four passive defenders without pausing (*Fig. 65*).
g) Beating four passive defenders, alternating left and then right or right and then left (*Figs. 66 and 67*).
h) Beating four defenders, who once again must remain anchored to the flag beind them. The player practising must beat the first defender on the left hand side (or right hand side) but he can choose to beat the second defender either on the left or the right (*Fig. 68*).

FIG. 65   FIG. 66   FIG. 67

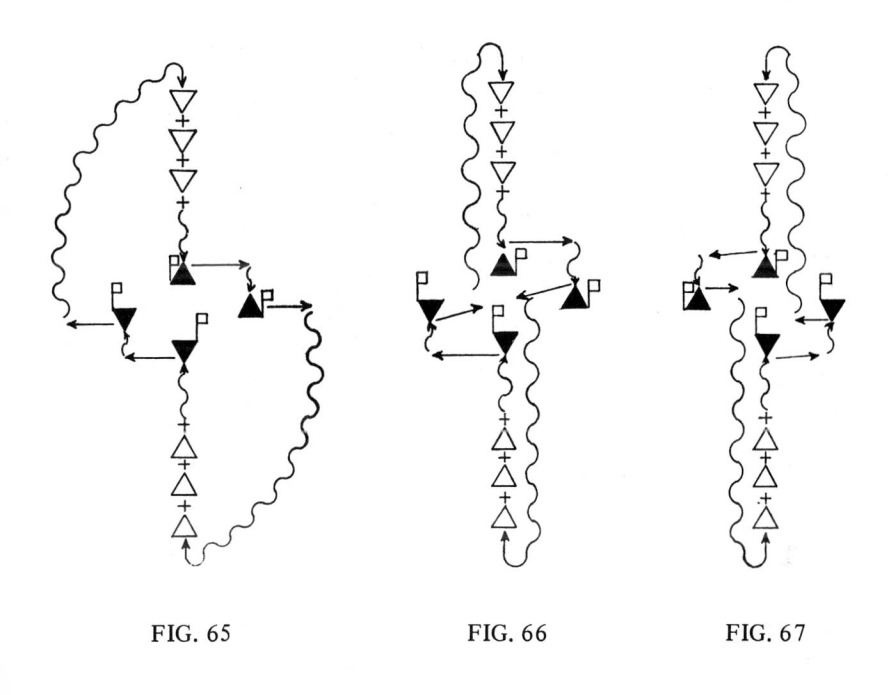

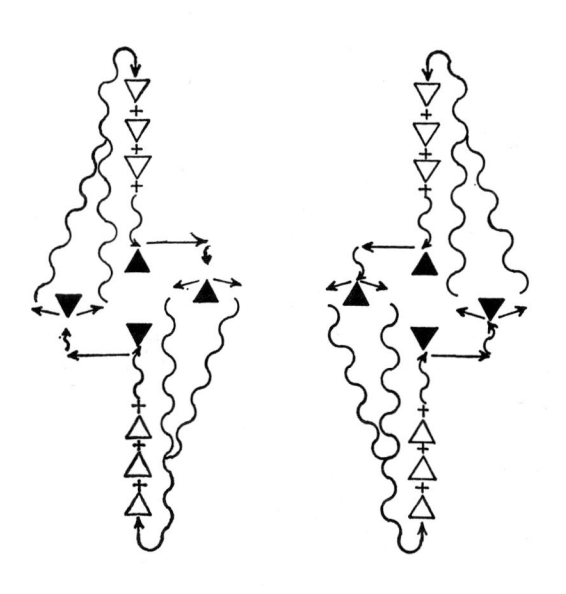

FIG. 68

4. **Beating an opponent with dummy moves**

   A particularly promising method of beating opponents for top-class players is to combine beating them on the left with beating them on the right (or *vice versa*).
   The player begins to beat his man on the left (or right) as described in 3 above. After having pushed the ball (and not dribbled as in 2 above) out of his opponent's reach, to the left (or right) he suddenly dodges off to the right (or left) immediately after having taken one pace sideways in the same direction as the ball, leaving aside the wrong-footed defender.

5. **Beating a defender introducing a stick dummy**

   While dribbling, the player suddenly pulls his stick over the top of the ball to one side, without in fact touching it.
   If the opponent is taken in by this deception, the player immediately takes the ball, which has been rolling straight on, to the opposite side. When beating an opponent on the right (left) hand side, the dribbler, immediately before pulling the ball across with the reverse stick (or with the stick in the normal position), should feint to move the ball to the left with the stick in the normal position (or to the right with the reverse stick).
   The stick dummy should be practised first when standing still and after when running with the ball towards an imaginary and passive opponent. (See 'Drill for practising the reverse stick stop' page 32 *et seq*). Finally the stick dummy should be practised in the standard combination 2 : 1 with the defender being active and unaware whether a dummy is to be carried out or not.

6. **Beating an opponent on the right (left) hand side coupled with a body swerve**

   (See 'The Dummy — an essential part of modern Technique and Tactics' page 88).

7. **Beating the right (left) hand side of an opponent by using a stick dummy and simultaneous body swerve**

   The player shifts the weight of his body in one direction, and at the same time, dummies with the stick in the same direction. By means of an abrupt push-off from his right (left) leg in the opposite direction, the forward pulls the ball to the right with the reverse stick (or conversely to the left) with the forehand in order to break free from his opponent, who, because he has been deceived, can only challenge again after some delay.

Drills for learning how to beat an opponent by means of a stick dummy and simultaneous body swerve:

a) The ball is placed 0.5m in front of the player. The stick dummy and simultaneous body-swerve are carried out first of all with the player stationary in front of a flag. In the first stage, the player passes the stick-head over the ball and moves his body to the same side. In the second stage, he sways in the opposite direction and pulls the ball to the right or left, as the case may be.
b) When practising the 'Indian dribble' (body, stick and ball should form a unit), the player intentionally misses out one touch carrying out this way the stick dummy and the body-swerve are carried out with a stationary ball in front of a flag.
c) When dribbling on the front stick the player dummies a pass to one side, combining a stick dummy and a body-swerve. The player must take care to begin his attempt at beating his opponent a good three metres in front of him; otherwise he will come into the defender's reach and run the risk of losing the ball.

Further methods of beating opponents are included in the Chapter 'The Dummy – an essential part of modern Technique and Tactics' page 88.

Beating an opponent is an art which not every player can master, especially because often there is a lack of experience and knowledge that the technique to be chosen depends on:
a) the part of the field where the manoeuvre is due to take place
b) the ground conditions
c) the position of the defender in relation to the attacker
d) the position of the defender in relation to his team-mates
e) the individual characteristics of the attacker
f) the physical or technical deficiencies of the defender
g) the methods of beating a man which the attacker has used before.

8 The Dummy - an Essential Part of Modern Technique and Tactics

The dummy is one of the most difficult and most effective aspects of hockey technique. The use of the dummy enriches a game, provides scope for invention and creates totally unexpected situations. There are very few other aspects of technique which provide a player with so much opportunity to exhibit his command of the game.

A dummy, or feint, is a movement designed to mislead the opponent, which does not produce the action it suggests. The player, for the purpose of concealing his true intentions, performs a certain action but does not carry it through, performing a different, and often quite contradictory, one.

There are many situations in the course of the game when a feint should be used in defence or attack to gain space or time for either passing or dribbling, by making the opponent go the wrong way. The dummy, therefore, in its most varied forms should be in every player's technical and tactical armoury. The more types of dummy a player has at his disposal and can use intelligently, the more dangerous he is to the opposition.

Nowadays the dummy is an essential part of modern technique and tactics. We differentiate here between feinting without the ball and feinting with the ball, which can be coupled with a body-swerve.

Feinting without the ball

Dummy manoeuvres without the ball (e.g. if the player abruptly stops while running or breaks into a run after standing still, or makes sudden changes of direction, or when trying to regain the possession of the ball steps forward and then suddenly backwards) are utilised either in order to break free of one's opponent or to force an opponent in possession of the ball to execute a movement for which the defender is already prepared. (See 'Lunging to tackle', page 128 and 'Tackling in retreat' page 130).

In order to get away from close marking, a player (for instance, a left inside) may use a body swerve, shifting his weight and dodging (say to the left), and drawing his opponent to move in the same direction. Immediately after the move to the left (the actual swerve); the player then moves suddenly and unexpectedly in his intended direction — the right, which gains him a slight and decisive advantage over his marker for receiving the pass from his centre-half in his reverse stick.

When carrying out a swerve, the player must make sure, among other things, that his centre of gravity does not move too violently to the side, as this only delays the second, or originally intended movement. It goes without saying that to use a body-swerve or a feint with the ball, is pointless when the opponent is still a long way off. The smaller the distance between the two opposing players, the more effective a feint becomes.

The most difficult form of body feint is the so called double body-swerve (which can also be performed with the ball). Initially the player moves as described above, but now misleads the opponent, after the first abrupt movement to the left, by dodging immediately afterwards to the right, only to return in a flash to the original direction in order to receive a pass. Apart from these methods of feinting, which can be used by all players in the course of the match, there are countless others. So, for example, the goalkeeper, when defending a penalty stroke, will incline his body to one side in order to induce the penalty-taker to flick the ball into the open corner of the goal, on which the goalkeeper's attention is actually concentrated. In order to create the best chances for a successful clearance, a defender will often, therefore, deliberately feint a lunge forward or to one or the other side. If a defender inclines the upper part of his body and places the stick to one side, he will frequently induce the forward dribbling towards him to play the ball to his other side. If the forward does in fact try to pass him on the inviting open side, the defender has achieved his aim. He will easily be able to deal with his opponent's action, as he is fully prepared for it.

Apart from playing catch, which is well suited to learning the body swerve (see 'Developing flexibility and dexterity' page 186), the two following exercises are recommended:

1. Running and body-swerving along a row of cones (distance between the cones about 15m). In front of each cone, the weight is perceptibly shifted to one side, and then pushed off powerfully from the outside leg; finally the player runs past the cone on the other side. The cones can also be replaced by players moving slowly forwards. The last player in the line swerves his way past the others and, having completed his run, takes his place at the head of the line.
2. Sidestepping coupled with a body-swerve, effected by a shift in weight.

   Two players stand opposite each other 10m apart on a straight line. One player after a quick sprint over the 10m, attempts to touch the player opposite; the latter sidesteps at the last moment with a sudden body feint or moves sideways with a double feint. Then the players change places.

Feinting with the ball and/or stick

Feinting with the ball and/or the stick is carried out by a player when dribbling in order to mislead his opponent. Mastery over this skill makes considerably greater demands on players than feinting with the body alone because the player must direct his attention, as he feints, not only to his opponent but also to the ball and/or stick. The most difficult, but most effective forms of feinting with the ball are those coupled with a stick dummy and body-swerve to mislead the opponent. In a match, only very well-trained players manage to produce these methods of feinting with any success.

As it would be a vain undertaking to try and describe all the various forms of feinting with the ball, only a few will be outlined here, as these are the most frequently used in matches.

1. The simplest method of feinting with the ball is to draw the ball sideways to the left (or right) at an angle to the line of the dribble, just in front of the opponent, so as to make the opponent sway to that side or even to take a few steps in that direction (*Fig. 56, 57, 62, 63*). If he does, then the forward immediately takes the ball past his opponent on the opposite side.
2. Beating an opponent with a body-swerve, produced by a shift of weight. (*See* page 86)
3. *Beating an opponent with a stick dummy* (*See* page 86)
4. Beating an opponent is to be seen in its most perfect form when coupled with a body swerve and a stick dummy, which is very deceptive. (*See* pages 86-87)
5. *Dummy passing.*
   The player suggests, for instance, by the appropriate backswing of his stick or by his stance or preparatory move, that he is going to pass (push pass, flick or hit) to the left. If the opponent attempts to prevent the ball being passed that way and alters his position in order to do so, the attacker pulls the ball back with his reverse stick and sets off to the right, past the man close to him. As with all the other types of dummy, this one, too, must appear genuine and convincing. (See also page 61 'Disguising the direction of the hit'.)
6. *Pulling the ball back:*
   Pulling the ball back, which is especially effective against a defender coming in from the side, is one of the most frequent methods of deceiving an opponent.
   While the player, for instance the outside left, dribbles the ball, his opponent runs in from the side. If the opponent goes for the dribbler, the latter returns the ball with the reverse stick, causing the opponent to

run on past, since he is unable to brake so quickly. In carrying this out, the dribbler must take care to see that he pulls the ball not directly backwards, but inside his right foot, to ensure that the opponent's stick will pass harmlessly out of reach of the ball. A pass normally follows this action but it can also develop into a rapid dribble into a gap towards the centre of the field.

7. *Variations on feinting to pull the ball back:*
The player in possession deliberately reduces his speed and stops the ball, so as to bring it close to his feet but still out of his opponent's reach. After stopping the ball this time, it is not passed but dribbled on again in the direction of the goal with a sudden burst of speed. The defender, who has just adjusted himself to the forward's reduced speed, will be unable to match the sudden burst of speed immediately, so that the player can gain a lead of a couple of metres and can break free of the man marking him.

8. Pulling the ball back as a means of deceiving the opposition is most brilliantly executed when the dribbler feints, while still running, to pull the ball back by means of a dummy reverse stick stop (*Fig. 69*). If during this stick dummy, the dribbler also sways a little backwards, as if to brake, but then accelerates with great suddenness after the stick dummy, he will certainly get past his opponent, who is now standing still in anticipation of his man pulling the ball back.

Fig. 69. Sloma of Germany feints to pull the ball back as Fokker of the Netherlands prepares to tackle. The author can just be seen behind Fokker

9. *Crossing the opponent's path:*
   Before the defender has a chance to tackle from side or behind (*Fig. 69*), the forward in possession should move suddenly sideways (*Fig. 70*), placing his body in front of the pursuing defender, who is forced to slow down.
10. *Competition using all these variations.*
    The player in possession starts from the centre line, followed by a defender about two metres behind him. Whilst the forward tries to reach the 22.90m line with the ball, or, after having gone at least six metres, returns to the centre line, the defender has to tackle and try to reach either line himself, having gained possession. On the way to either line, the forward may apply any feint of pulling the ball back or crossing the opponent's path.

During the match the player should vary as much as possible the above methods of feinting, so as to increase his opponent's feeling of uncertainty. The defender, in fact, should never be able to anticipate which dummy the dribbler will use and the forward should always be unaware about the type of tackling the defender will apply.

Fig. 70. Garraffo of Argentina crosses his opponent's path too late for an effective tackle

A player using the same tricks each time causes no problem for the opposition. The success of a dummy depends not only on the perfect execution of the movement but also on the well-chosen alternation of its various forms. A player who knows many types of dummy and can use them flexibly according to each situation is superior to other players and will always present a riddle for the man marking him, as the defender never knows which skill the forward is about to use.

The above movements should not be carried out too quickly or else the opponent will be unable to register them and react. If, however, they are carried out too slowly, the opponent can see through them and will not be taken in. Either way the point of deception will be lost.

The attacker or defender who is skilful in employing the dummy can shake the poise and self-confidence of his opponent by a successful feint and furthermore can undermine the sureness of the whole opposing defence or attacking line. As the opponent's unsureness increases, so the self-confidence of the attacker (defender) rises proportionately, if he succeeds in fooling his opponent with a dummy. For just this reason, forwards (defenders) should try some sort of dummy on their assigned opponent at their first encounter.

To sum up, it can be said that the dummy has proved itself to be a particularly effective aspect of technique and tactics when used with variety, at the correct moment according to the situation and in the interest of the game as a whole.

9 Tactical Exercises to Improve the Combined Attack

A comparison between the goals scored in games before and after 1978 leads one inevitably to wonder about today's bigger score-lines. Besides hockey being exclusively played on natural grass before 1978 the small number of goals scored in every match was largely due to the fact that the defence had learned new tactics, thus making a successful penetration into the circle more difficult for the forwards.* The centre-half adopted a less attacking role than in the 50's and 60's. The backs generally intercepted their opponents well before the 22.90m line and not on the edge of the circle. The inside forwards paid more attention to defence, when the other side was in possession and exceptionally dangerous forwards were frequently blotted out by the excellence of the close marking. Since, moreover, speed and stamina, as well as power and skill — qualities mainly possessed in early days only by forwards — were to be found among defenders as well, an attacking movement was far less likely to be brought to a successful conclusion as the basic rules of attack were not applied. Here are some of the most important basic rules in attack to be considered:
— move the opposing defender
— support the player in possession of the ball
— assure width and depth in order to gain more time and space for the attack
— pass the ball in the very right moment
— dictate the rhythm
— change the direction of the attack quickly
— assure unpredictability and variety
— try to gain for some seconds a numerical advantage of attacking players in relation to the number of opposing defenders
— prefer counter attacks to positional attacks because of their higher effectiveness
— maintain pressure on the defender not to allow him to develop his game
— look systematically after a shot at the opponent's goal for a rebound.

Methods of defence have developed successfully, especially in the 60's and 70's, whereas forward play has only recently followed suit and adapted

---

* see 'The Advanced Science of Hockey' chapter — 'The development from zonal and man-to-man marking to combined marking'

to altered circumstances. The vain efforts of the attack against tactically superior defenders have caused the press to reiterate the comment appropriate to most matches: 'the defence in both teams was outstanding'. To try and redress the balance and to put teeth back into the attack, the following reflections seem pertinent: In modern hockey interpassing rarely involves only two players. It is true that, to the casual glance, only two players seem to be combining but, looking at the game more attentively, it becomes obvious that successful combined play results from the mutual assistance of several players.

Since defenders deny front players time and space, it follows that time and space have to be created tactically, otherwise successful combined play, particularly in attack, can be seen in very few teams. Unfortunately most players do not know how to create time and space or they simply do not have the requisite abilities. The main abilities are that the players can receive and control the ball in any situation and arriving at any speed, know how to pass the ball accurately, at the correct moment and at the correct pace; above all, the receivers should possess the physical fitness to be able continually to move into the open spaces and make themselves available for a pass.

Swopping positions or leaving a position unoccupied are aspects of modern attacking play which confuse the opposition and constitute a tactical means to make defence more difficult. By this we mean that the players deliberately, and for tactical reasons, depart from their appointed position in the original team formation and offer their area of play to another player.

Changing positions demands:
1. Increased fitness, both mental and physical, from the individual players.
2. That each player of the team is able to play effectively for some time in any position in the field.
3. That the players should understand in theory the real importance of swopping positions. They must be shown, by clear examples, when and how positions should be swopped. Apart from the theory, very simple practices for combined movements should be introduced first, which become more and more difficult later on, until the players begin to realise, on their own initiative, when to interchange or offer positions during the game according to the situation. (*See* chapter 12 in *The Advanced Science of Hockey*)

A basic condition for the forwards who frequently leave their appointed areas in the field is they should not only interchange in the width of the field but also, and more especially, in the depth. A forward who leaves his position creates a free space which one of his team-mates may penetrate suddenly from behind confronting the opponent defence with a whole host of tactical problems.

Initially, the forwards should swop positions only occasionally but later, encouraged by their successes, more and more players should rotate, so as to increase the defence's feeling of uncertainty. The use of this tactic, to improve the effectiveness of the forward play, becomes more and more important in proportion to the speed of the covering defence. The following graduated drills should be of assistance in improving general understanding of combined play in attack.

In this, most attention is to be directed at general coaching, without forgetting, however, to go into the individual positions. All the movements suggested can, therefore, be tried out irrespective of the positions normally occupied by individual members of the team.

1.
a) *Combined movements with square passes in pairs.*
b) *Square passing between flags.*
Six flags are placed along the length of a pitch. Two players, about eight metres apart, run either side of the line of flags keeping parallel to them. A dribbles the ball until midway between the first two flags, when he passes the ball square through the flags to B (*Fig. 71*).

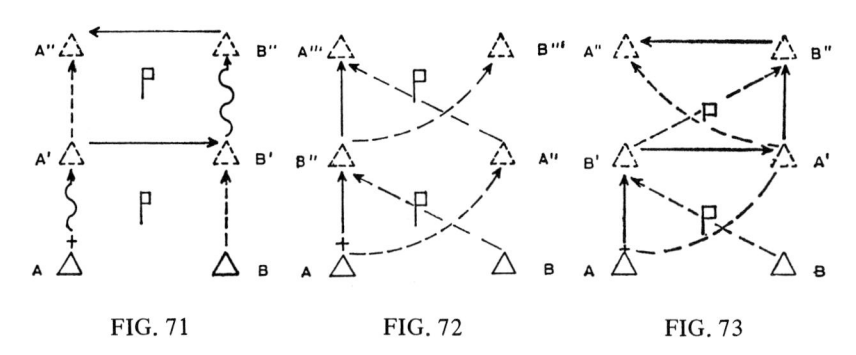

FIG. 71   FIG. 72   FIG. 73

The latter dribbles until midway between the second and third flag, when he passes without any time consuming preparation square to A who is running into position to receive the ball (see 'Drills for practising the reverse stick stop on the run' page 34).
c) The same with a disguised square pass and later on with a passive defender.

2.
a) *Through passing in pairs without flags.*
b) *Through passing with flags as imaginary opponents.*
Flags at approximately 15m intervals, are placed along a straight line.

After two players give each other well-timed passes and swop positions. B runs onto a through pass from A, level with the midpoint between the first two flags, and plays the ball on again immediately in the same direction (*Fig. 72*). Care must be taken to avoid obstructing the imaginary opponent.

c) The same with a disguised through pass and later on with a passive defender.

3.
a) *Through and square passes without flags.*
b) *Through and square passes, using flags as imaginary opponents.*

Two players start from the goal line and alternate between giving through passes when they reach one flag and then square passes through the next two flags.

After passing, each player immediately runs into position for the next pass (*Fig. 73*). A gives only through passes, B only square passes. On the return the roles are changed.

c) The same, with disguised through passes.
d) The same, with disguised square passes.
e) Free choice of through and square passes without and with passive defender.

4.
a) *Dribbling into another position followed by a square pass ('Switch').*
I.L. dribbles the ball to the L.W. position and then gives a square pass to the right, where the L.W. has run into position from behind him. Now it is the L.W.'s turn, after having observed that the I.L. offered his position.

Dribbling into another position, followed by a square pass, is especially successful when the opposing team marks closely. (*Fig. 74*).

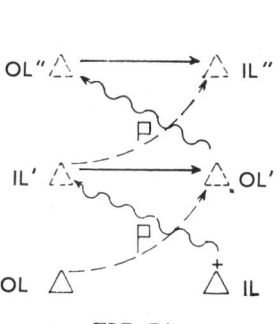

FIG. 74 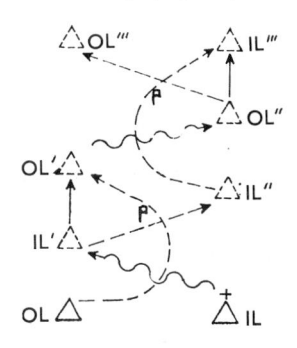   FIG. 75

b) The same with a passive defender, who follows the attacker in possession of the ball. Only when the defender was moved out of his position should the square pass be played out of his reach to the other attacker, who continues to practise another 'switch'.
c) Dribbling diagonally to the right with a square pass to the left. In the exercises 5-14 the flags are placed at 20m intervals.

5.
a) *Dribbling into another position followed by a through pass.*
b) The same with flags. The first player dribbles into the new position diagonally in front of the flag and gives a through pass for the other player (*Fig. 75*), who sprints with a change of speed into the free space. He should take care always to run behind the back of the dribbler and equally, behind the back of the opponent (here the flags) on his way to the ball to avoid a third party obstruction.
c) The same with a disguised through pass, and later on with a passive defender.

6.
a) *Dribbling into position with through and square passes.*
The I.L. dribbles the ball into the L.W. position and then gives a through pass which the L.W. runs on to and returns as a square pass to the I.L. (*Fig. 76*).
b) The same with disguised through passes.

7. *Dribbling into position with a square pass followed by a through pass.* (*Fig. 77*).

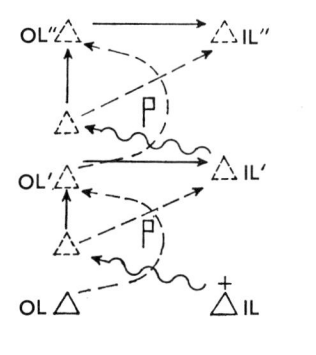

FIG. 76 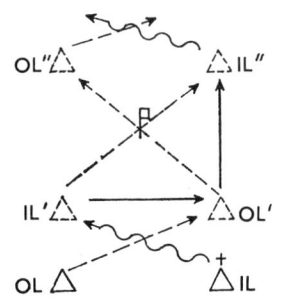　　　　　　　　　FIG. 77a

Fig. 77b. 2 : 1 situation in the India-Pakistan match, 1983, in Karachi.

8. *Free combination.*
a) Combined movements in pairs involving the free choice of dribbling into position, square passing and through passing.
b) Combined movements in pairs with a free choice of techniques against one defender (*Fig. 77b*) protecting a goal 15m wide. Either of the attackers must actually dribble the ball over the line to score. (see '*The Advanced Science of Hockey*' pages 94-98)

9.
a) *Square passing with three players.*
All the players run level in a line and square pass the ball to each other. Care should be taken to perfect the reception of the ball coming from the left or right and to give as soon as the ball is controlled an effective pass.
b) The same. One player, who is not in possession, sprints away from the line. The ball is then passed to the other player who remains level with the passer. One forward is always forced, therefore, to run into position in vain.

10. *Through passes with three players.*
A gives a through pass to B, who had offered himself before A passed. After receiving the ball and connecting visually with C he gives a through pass to C. A and C run into the positions shown in Fig. 78.

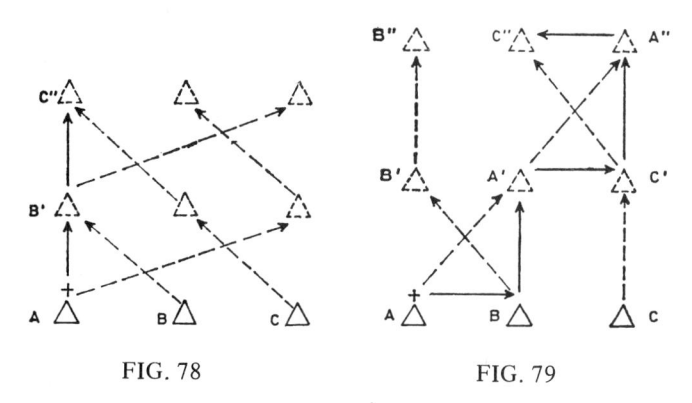

FIG. 78   FIG. 79

11.
a) *Combined play between three players, alternating square passes and through passes.*
A gives only square passes and runs onto through passes from B and C (*Fig. 79*).
Each player must have one turn at giving only square passes.
b) *Combined play between three players, alternating through passes and square passes.*
A gives only through passes and runs on to square passes from B and C (*Fig. 80*).
Each player must have one turn at giving only through passes.

12. *Combined movements between three players using a free choice of through and square passes.*
One of the two forwards not in possession must always make himself available for a through pass, so that the three forwards are never in a line. Only when the one forward has moved out of position does the pass result, in the form of either a through pass or a square pass.

13. *Combined movements between three players : dribbling into position and giving a square pass.*
The player in the middle always dribbles the ball to one side or the other, followed by a square pass to the player with whom he has just switched position (*Fig. 81*).

FIG. 80   FIG. 81

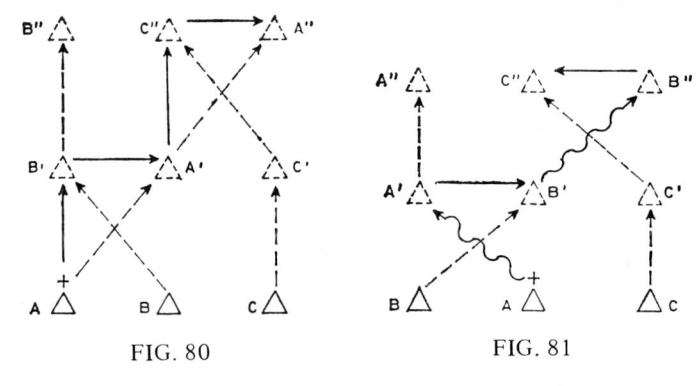

14. *Free combination between three players using dribbling into position, square passing and through passing.*

15. *Combined play between three players against a defender.*
    The attackers must dribble the ball over a line 15m long. There is no off-side. They should be aware of third party obstruction (see pages 106-108).

16.
a) *Combined play between three players against two defenders* (see pages 109-110). The goal is now increased to 20m.
b) *The same in front of the circle with a goal-keeper.*

17.
a) *Free combination of a wing pair against a wing-half who defends a goal 12m wide.*
   The I.L. is in possession; his task is to bring the L.W. into the game. The I.L. can do this in three possible ways.
   1. The square pass
   2. The through pass (also using a flick) and
   3. A switch (dribbling into the L.W. position followed by a square pass).
b) *The same.* As the wing half in a) above was constantly being beaten, his task should now be made easier. The R.H. should always mark the player at that moment in the L.W. position. He must not take on the forward in the I.L. position unless that player runs into the L.W. position. A goal (that is to say, dribbling the ball across a goal-line 12 metres long) can now be scored only by the winger.

18. *Combined movements between two forwards against two defenders.*

The forwards attack from the centre line in order to get into the circle against the opposition of two defenders, one of them hanging back about 10m. The two forwards should make use of all the variations which they have learned in the preceding exercises, including beating an opponent. Frequently the forward without the ball stays back on purpose to engage his defender, so that the other forward can run diagonally into the gap with the ball, introducing a 'switch'.

19.
a) *Combined play in the form of a moving triangle.*
The L.W. (R.W.) I.L. (I.R.) and L.H. (R.H.) or a mid-field player practise the move on a full-size pitch. The forwards give only square or back passes and take care never to move closer than 6m to each other.
Other triangles of three players can also practise in opposite directions at the same time on the same side of the pitch.
b) The same. The two forwards alternate between giving square, through and back passes. They swop positions frequently, whereas the wing-half, or mid-field player, remains in his position.
c) The same. Now the three players should change positions (rotation), with the triangular formation always maintained. The movement starts always with the player in possession of the ball dribbling into a position vacated by one of his team-mates. The rotation should be executed in both directions.

20. *Combined play in a moving triangle against one opponent.*
The attackers combine against one active opponent between centre and 22.90m line with the aim to carry the ball across a 10m goal-line within six to eight seconds.

21.
a) *Combined play of three forwards against two active opponents within a square of 12m.*
How many passes can be played without losing the ball to the two defenders? More exercises for the standard combination 3 : 2 are given on page 109 and especially in '*The Advanced Science of Hockey*' pages 102-106.

22.
a) *Combined play in the form of a moving triangle when two players are closely marked.*
The wing half after having achieved a mutual agreement with his marked

forward gives a skilful pass to one of his forwards, so that the forward without obstructing the defender can take possession of the ball, beat individually, or with the help of his team-mates, the defence in order to cross the 22.90m line with the ball (the attacking side scores a point). If the combination is intercepted, the defence scores a point. The wing half can dribble the ball but he cannot score a point for his team.

b) The same. The previous exercise can also be extended in scope by making the defenders concentrate on marking the players in the triangle who form the spearhead of the attack very tightly. The attacking players should find out for themselves at least four movements for avoiding the effectiveness of man-to-man marking.

23. *The follow-up* (Fig. 82):

Two forwards build up a fast attack starting from the centre line, followed by a defender who starts 2m behind them at the moment the first forward plays the ball. This is the movement seen in the match photograph, *Fig. 82.*

To force the forwards to speed up their game, the following practices are recommended (see also '*The Advanced Science of Hockey*', 'The Theory and Practice of Counter-attacks'):

Fig. 82. A fast attack from Poland in a Test match against France in 1977

24. *Attacking against the clock.*
a) Three forwards have to beat one back. The forwards start off from the centre-line; they must then aim at beating the back as quickly as possible in order to get in a shot at goal. Every forward must touch the ball at least once. Several groups of three forwards can compete with each other and the winning group is the one that achieves the best average time for its runs within a certain period.
b) Two forwards to one defender.
c) Four to two.

25 *Contest between the forwards, a half, and a defender:*
a) Two players start from the centre-line. 3m behind them is a half-back, who has already been beaten and passed, and who, with the help of one back, has to stop the three forwards. When the whistle goes, the forwards start off and, by quick interpassing, try to beat the back and score a goal without being caught by the half who has set off at the same time. If the half succeeds in catching them up, then the forwards' advantage is lost. If they shoot at goal before the half catches them, they score one point with two for scoring a goal. If the half does catch up the forwards, then the defence scores a point, as it does also for a successful tackle. The team with the most points after a specified time is the winner.
b) Three attackers to one defender and a half.
c) Four attackers to two defenders and a half.
d) Five to three and one half with off-side.
e) Four to three; watch for off-side.

26. All these tactical games with the ratio of forwards to defenders of three to one, three to two, four to two, five to three or three to three with an extra neutral players, help to improve the formation of combined play and, furthermore, help to practise the players in moving into the open spaces. (*See* 'Running into the open space' page 105).

In all these practices, attention must be paid to the precise moment and the accuracy of each pass. Through these exercises the ball carrier should learn to 'read' how the players around him will react, to pass the ball rather than be enticed into taking on an opponent and to look for and play those passes demanded by the team tactics.

Fast, mobile and skilful defenders have made the task of the forwards more difficult than before, because the forwards are also required to work hard defensively when their opponents have the ball. However when the attackers learn and understand the language of passing (when, how or where the ball should be psssed especially with close marking), then more goals than ever before are likely to be scored!

10 Running into the Open Space

The attitude that has been prevalent since hockey's earliest days is that it is the man in possession who determines the moment, the direction and the speed of the pass; this needs correction if the level of hockey is to be raised.

Today's hockey player should be fully aware that it is not the man in possession but the players moving into the open spaces that give any combined movement its impetus (*Fig. 83a*).

It is not the man with the ball but the receiver running free
— to receive the ball directly
— to create space for himself
— to create space into which a team-mate may run free
— to create space into which a team-mate may dribble
— to create space into which the ball may be passed for a team-mate who thereby determines the direction and speed of the pass by the direction he has taken and by the speed at which he is running.

Misunderstandings between individual players which frequently occur as for example when
a) the receiver does not want the ball, because he is tired, out of position or simply not ready
b) the receiver does not signal with his body movements, his stick position and through eye-contact with the player in possession of the ball when, where and how the ball should be passed to him
c) the passer wrongly assesses a match situation and passes to the wrong position
d) the passer makes a wrong decision because of lack of experience and tactical knowledge
e) the passer is unable, due to lack of skill, to make a pass
f) the player passes the ball too hard or too soft due to a wrong optical-physical assessment
g) the pass is badly timed, usually too late
h) the pass is not disguised, and can be easily anticipated
i) the receiver waits for the ball instead of running to it
can be eliminated to a great extent by heeding this tactical advice.

Systematic movement into the open space, hitherto practised insufficiently in training, demands, quite apart from considerable physical qualities, mental agility and rapid powers of decision. These qualities must be acquired by suitable types of practice. Especially suitable for learning how to move into

Fig. 83a. F.L. Poon (Malaysia) offers himself in the centre forward position for a pass to his front stick. (Malaysia-Canada in the Olympic Games in Montreal)

the open space are the 'cat and mouse' games used with three forwards against one defender, two against one, three against two, four against two, four against three and five against four. Few of them will be explained here, as all of them are described systematically in *The Advanced Science of Hockey* pages 86-107.

1. 3 : 1
a) *Three forwards against one defender for practice in diagonal passing.*
Three players, in not too large an area (10m × 10m), pass the ball among themselves trying to avoid one active opponent. So that the player in possession always has a chance of passing safely to either side, his two colleagues without the ball must run off the ball after each pass, in such a way that one of them is always to be found on either side of the player in possession of the ball.

If the defender touches the ball, he then swops places with the forward.

Basic tactical attitudes for the ball carrier which players should heed when the ratio of attackers to defenders is as above and also when playing two against one, three against two and four against two, are:
— Before you pass to a well-positioned colleague you must draw an opponent so as to take him out of the game.

- Do not dribble the ball too near to your opponent or he will stand a good chance of picking up your pass.
- Do not remain inactive after your pass but immediately run into an open space.

The following suggestions are of value for the other forwards supporting the man in possession.

- The two colleagues who move into the open spaces, must do so in such a way that the dribbler can always find a player to either side of him ready for the pass.
- Place yourself level with the ball or even better a little behind it, ready for a square pass; do not place yourself in front of the ball, otherwise, in certain circumstances, you will force the man in possession to give a diagonal pass which can easily be picked up by the defender.

The defender should try to induce mistakes from the three forwards by feinting to tackle and by retreating in defence.

b) *Three against one, attacking a small goal with a goal-keeper.*

Goals can be scored from either side. The goal-keeper who, together with the defender, makes up the defending team is not allowed to leave the goal-line.

c) *Three against one, with a wide goal.*

Three forwards attempt to beat one defender, standing eight to ten metres in front of a goal ten metres wide, in such a way that one of them manages to dribble the ball over the goal-line. After eight attacks have been mounted, one of the forwards takes the defender's place and the latter becomes a forward. Who was the most successful defender during the course of his eight attacks?

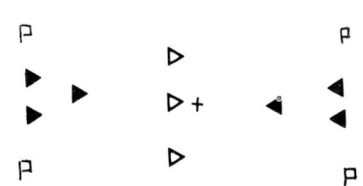

FIG. 83b

d) *Three against one, with three teams (Fig. 83b).*

Three teams, each with three active players, play on a pitch 22.90m long; one team attacks either of two goals, which are 20m wide, defended by the other two teams. If either defending side succeeds in winning the ball for three seconds, either through their defender or their two goal-keepers (who are not allowed to leave the goal-line), they cease to be the defending side; they then attack the goal opposite, while the previous attackers, after losing the ball, take up their position with one man out and two goal-keepers in the goal which they themselves have just unsuccessfully attacked.

A goal can be scored when an attacker manages to cross the goal line with the ball. A goal does not count, however, if the ball is hit.

Which team after ten minutes has been able to score the most goals? It is a good idea to differentiate between the three sides by having them wear different coloured shirts.

The above game is made more difficult, if the attacking side is allowed only eight seconds for bringing the attack to its conclusion. If they have not been able to score a goal in this time, the defending side automatically gets the ball and the turn to attack.

Variation: Three against one, with three teams, playing into regular goals defended by two goalkeepers staying on the goal line.

2. 2 : 1
a) *Two against one, attacking a wide goal*
   As only one colleague is available to pass to, he must constantly endeavour to create gaps for the man in possession by his running into the open space. The player with the ball must keep an eye on the opponent the whole time to decide from his opponent's actions, as well as those of his partner, whether to give a square or through pass, or whether he should try to reach the goal-line by dribbling through himself. If he runs into an open space immediately after passing, this makes the defender's task more difficult.
b) One against one, attacking two small goals with a neutral player who always plays in the side of the man in possession.
c) Two against one, with three teams changing around.
   Line-up as in 1.d), except that now two forwards play against one defender and one 'goal-keeper'.

3. 4 : 2
a) *Four against two.*
   This time the player in possession has three partners, two of whom run off the ball, so as to be in a position to receive a safe pass.
   The third takes up his position at the end of a 'channel' formed by

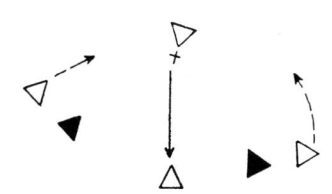

FIG. 83c

the position of two defenders. Since the two defenders can normally mark only two players, the ball can be played to the third unmarked partner (*Fig. 83c*). With the four against two combination the player in possession gets used to looking for the pass into the gap, whereas a defender learns to screen off the open space.

b) Four against two, attacking a goal 4m wide with a goal-keeper. The goal can be attacked from either side. A defender must remain in defence until he manages to get possession of the ball for three seconds. The forward losing the ball changes with the defender.

c) Ball over the line with three teams.
Three teams play across the pitch from side-line to side-line. Between the 22.90m line and the centre line, the side-lines of the normal pitch act as goal-lines, over which the players are to dribble the ball. Two teams, each with two players, defend their goal-line, while a third team, in midfield with four players, attacks for two minutes. After each goal, or the repulse of an attack, the ball is immediately returned to the attacking side and they immediately start a new attack on the opposite goal-line. There is no off-side.

After two minutes all four defenders go into attack and the four attackers should split into two teams of two defenders. The workload can be varied at will by lengthening or reducing the playing time.

4. 3 : 2
a) *Three against two.*
This practice game comes very close to match conditions for, in modern hockey, three players frequently work closely together; the wing pair, for example, with their wing-half, or the sweeper with the centre-half and one of the wing-halves. The two attackers, who are running off the ball, should continually set up opportunities for their colleagues in possession to be able to pass the ball. When a pass from one of the three within the 12m square has been intercepted by a defender, the two players involved change round. Good sense of perspective and mutual understanding between the forwards make it much more difficult for the two defenders to intercept the ball. Dribbling is allowed at first but later the players may touch the ball only twice before passing.

b) Three against two, attacking a 4m goal with a goal-keeper (without pads).
As in 3.b) or with the following variation. The change-round between the attacking and defending sides is made when the defenders succeed in passing the ball twice running among themselves (including the goal-keeper). The side with the most goals at the end of the specified time is the winner.

c) Taking the ball over the line with three teams.
   As in 3.c) The team in mid-field attacks for two minutes with three forwards and a defence consisting of two defenders.
d) Two against two attacking two wide goals with a neutral player always assisting the side in possession.
e) Three against two with three teams changing round.
   As in 1.d) except that the defence now plays with one goalkeeper and two defenders, instead of with two goal-keepers and one defender.

5. Four against three.
   How many seconds can the four players in possession manage to keep the ball among themselves? How many passes are they able to make before losing possession of the ball.

6. Three against three, with and without a neutral player.
a) Three against three (also four against four) play against small goals across the width of a hockey pitch. To add fluency to the game, first a neutral player who has no direct opponent could be added. He always plays on the side of the team in possession of the ball and so gives it a numerical superiority.
b) The game can also be played using goals 22.90m wide instead of small goals. A goal is then scored when a player dribbles the ball over his opponent's goal-line. The neutral player changes sides every three minutes and not every time the ball is lost.
   (For tactical explanations see the chapter 'The tactics of passing' and in 'The Advanced Science of Hockey' pp. 86-107).

7. Two sides and three goals.
a) Two sides each with three or four players try to get the ball through any one of three goals which are placed between the 22.90m line and the centre line (Fig. 84). Each pass through the goal, which can be picked up by another player on the same side, scores one point.

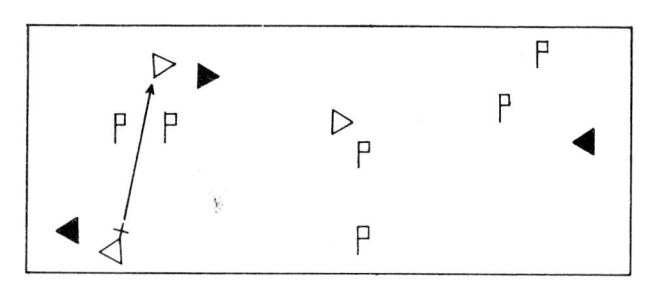

FIG. 84

As each player has a definite opponent, the art of passing, movement into the open space, marking a man and also each player's ability to change speed and direction with and without ball are practised in this game.

All players must pay constant attention to the various possibilities which develop with regard to the build-up before a goal and the actual scoring of a goal.

b) All goals are placed on the 22.90m line.

8. *Ten passes.*

Two teams each with four players, playing in an area bounded by the centre-line, 22.90m line and side-lines, attempt to keep the ball as long as possible among themselves. The side having just lost the ball makes every effort to intercept their opponents' passes who, for their part, try to achieve as many passes as possible. For each successful pass to a colleague one point is scored. The winning side is the one which first achieves ten consecutive passes.

The idea of the game, that is scoring a number of points by accurate passing, forces the players in the side having possession to run into the open spaces, to play off the ball, and to give fast, accurate passes as well as compelling their opponents to mark closely. The players' task is made more difficult if they are allowed to hold the ball for only five seconds or easier if the defending team can only field three players, or is not allowed to mark closely.

9. Names.

Attackers in numerical superiority (4 : 3) attempt to pass the ball among themselves in an order given by the coach who calls the name of the receiver. When the attackers manage to achieve four passes without losing possession of the ball, they and the defenders change their functions.

Giving the pass and immediate movement into the open space

An important characteristic of modern hockey is the requirement that the player should immediately run into an open space after giving a successful pass.

In general, running into an open space and, in particular, the immediate movement into an open space after giving the pass, form the basis for fluid combined play and are a necessary condition for the achievement of numerical superiority, which is especially difficult to achieve close to the opposing circle. The sudden assault, which develops in a flash from a defensive position generally beginning with an accurate and quick pass, is one of the most important weapons to avoid – the effectiveness of close marking. Players, who remain in their own position after a successful pass, have not completely fulfilled their task. Following their pass they should immediately run into the open space in anticipation of receiving a pass back. Also a defender should show his attacking spirit in this way.

Training hints: Movement into the open space after giving a pass must be assisted by appropriate simple tasks during practice games, in the course of basic hockey training, in such a way that the player becomes conscious of its tactical significance as he carries it out. The relationship between the pass and running off the ball can easily be made automatic during the coaching of the push and the hit.

Movement into the open space should be linked with a sudden change of speed immediately after the pass, or even while playing the ball. Therefore a player should be set the task of covering the first 5 or 6m at a sprint after every pass. The accuracy of the pass must not, however, suffer from the player sprinting away immediately.

Drills.
1. Three players stand at three corners of a square. A passes left to B and runs off to the right to the unoccupied corner (*Fig. 85*). B then plays the ball to C and sets off to the now unoccupied corner etc. Therefore whereas the ball is always passed to the left, the players always run off the ball to the right.
2. Three players occupy three corners of a square. B plays the ball diagonally to player A, who is standing opposite him, and runs to the unoccupied corner of the square (*Fig. 86*).

    A now passes to C, who up until now has only been watching, and then runs diagonally to B's previous position.

    Whoever receives the ball diagonally, gives a square pass. Whoever receives the ball from his nearest partner, passes it diagonally to the

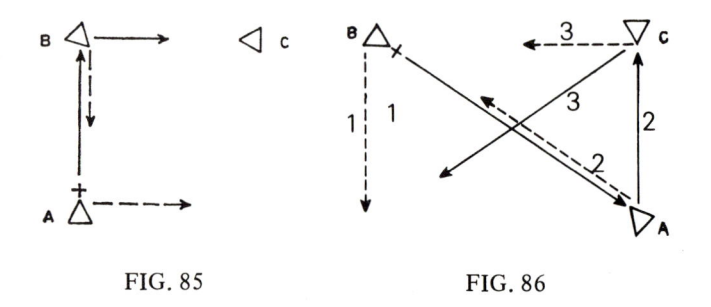

FIG. 85   FIG. 86

player standing opposite. After each pass, the player immediately sprints to the unoccupied corner of the square.
3. Three players occupy three corners of a square with sides of 10-15m. The ball is always placed to the empty corner of the square (Fig. 87), after eye contact is made between passer and receiver.

The passer must always run to the position of the player who started off just after the ball. Therefore the pass is to the unoccupied position and running off into the position being vacated.

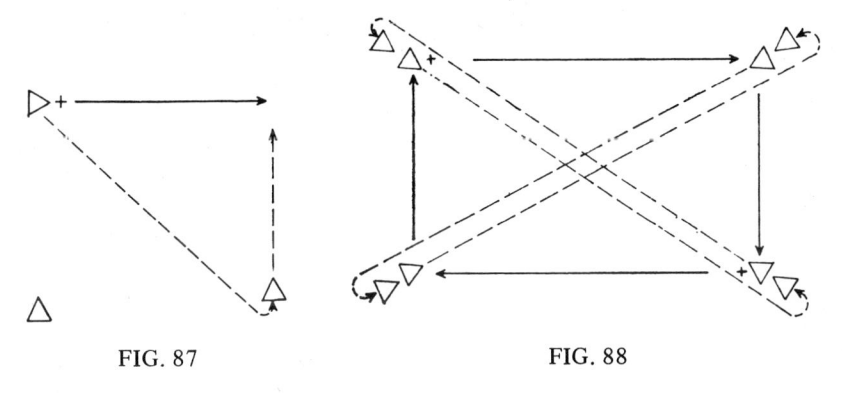

FIG. 87   FIG. 88

4. Two players stand at each corner of a rectangle or square (*Fig. 88*). The two balls being used in this game are always passed to the left. After each pass the player concerned sprints to the end of the group standing diagonally opposite.

The runner must always be in his new group before the ball.
5. Each corner of the square has two players standing at it. The two balls are with the opposite groups (*Fig. 89*). The first players of these two groups dribble the ball to the middle of the square where they pass it to

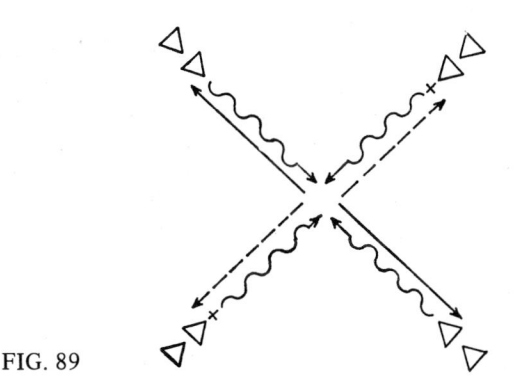

FIG. 89

the left (or right). After the pass the player immediately runs off straight ahead.

Further drills for the immediate movement off the ball after a pass are to be found in the following chapters: — 'The Hit' page 40, 'Tactical Exercises to Improve the Attack' page 94, and 'The Methodical development of the wall-pass and first-time pass' in *The Advanced Science of Hockey* pp. 79-81. Triangular pass play between two players also depends on the practical application of the tactical recommendation of immediately running into position after the pass.

Methodical development of the triangular pass

The wall pass which very often is a triangular pass is a means of passing the ball between two players to eliminate a defender. When the oncoming ball has sufficient speed, it is best to deflect the ball to a team mate who may be moving past. The wall, first time, direct, triangular or deflected pass has an increased importance in modern artificial turf hockey. The higher the level of play of one's team, the more this technical-tactical skill is used.

1. *Simple triangular play.*
a) After the pass from player A to the right into the forehand of player B, B plays the ball into A's path and then runs to the other side of the flag. There B makes himself ready for another triangular pass after a pass from A (*Figs. 90/91*). The pass to the right is the most common and most effective initial pass for triangulation. Before passing with the front stick or reverse-stick on the run, the passer should have observed the position of his team-mate as well as the position and the movements of the defender. The triangular pass should be played first time with the right hand gripping the stick lower down the handle than usual, with the trunk in the moment of impact in a 45° position with the head over the ball and with the stick in a horizontal position (on artificial turf) and on natural grass in an almost vertical position to avoid the ball bouncing over the head of the stick. Instead of playing the ball with the initial part of the curve as on natural grass, on artificial turf the ball should touch the stick very close to the position of the right hand in the centre of the stick. During the execution of the first-time triangular pass both legs should be bent sufficiently in order to bring the point of gravity lower to the ground which gives the passer better vision and enables him to react more readily to the next move.
b) After the square pass from A to B to the right on the first run or to the left on the return run (second phase), the ball without being stopped is passed back for A to run on to (Fig. 92/93).

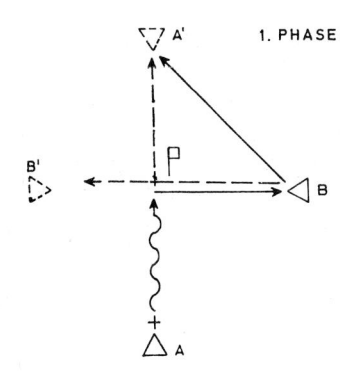

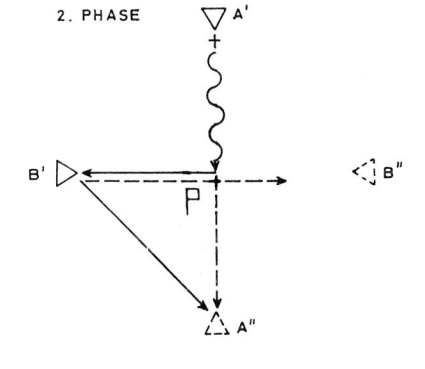

FIG. 90

FIG. 91

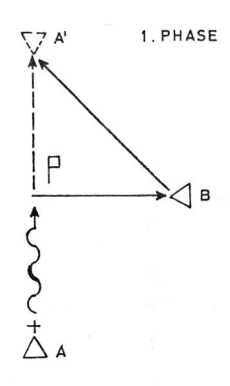

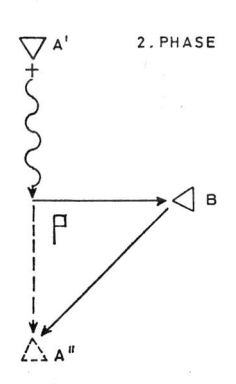

FIG. 92

FIG. 93

Whereas A always runs up and down along a straight line and gives square passes to the right or left, B, in contrast to a) above, always remains in the same position.

c) Both players stand level with each other about 6m away from the flag. There should be about 6m between the two partners. Maintaining this distance, the two players run towards the flag. Immediately before reaching it B receives a square pass from A into his forehand. B, without stopping while on the run, gives a diagonal triangular pass for A to run on to (Fig. 94). When the latter regains possession, he turns round and begins the triangulation again from the other side. Whereas A always initiates the triangulation and is also in possession again at the end, B always executes the wall pass with his forehand.

d) The same with a passive defender.

FIG. 94a — 1. PHASE

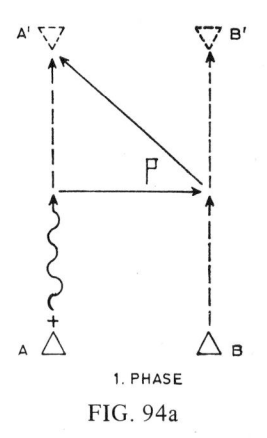

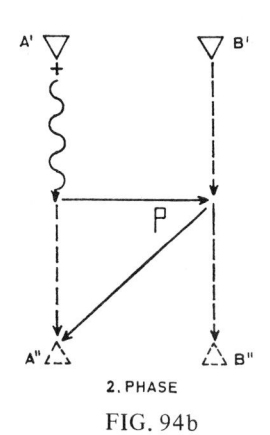

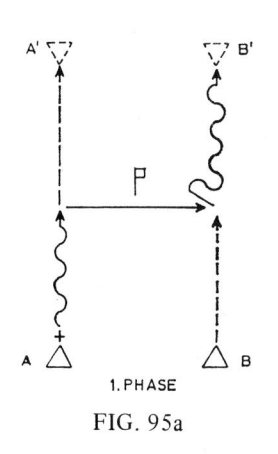

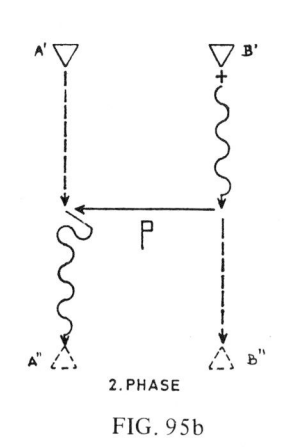

FIG. 94b — 2. PHASE

FIG. 95a — 1. PHASE

FIG. 95b — 2. PHASE

2. *Dummy triangulation.*

a) After the initial square pass from A to B, B dummies a wall pass (a diagonal pass to the left) for A to run on to but then leaves his position quickly to move off to the right and pass his opponent (the flag but later a passive defender), who is expecting a triangular pass, on the right side (*Fig. 95*).

b) After the square pass from B to A, A dummies, a wall pass to the right for B to run on to, then moves rapidly away from his position, passing the flag (the passive defender) on the left (*Fig. 96*).

3. *Triangulation with the players swopping positions.*

a) A second form of triangular pass which, in contrast to the first, hardly

FIG. 96a 1. PHASE

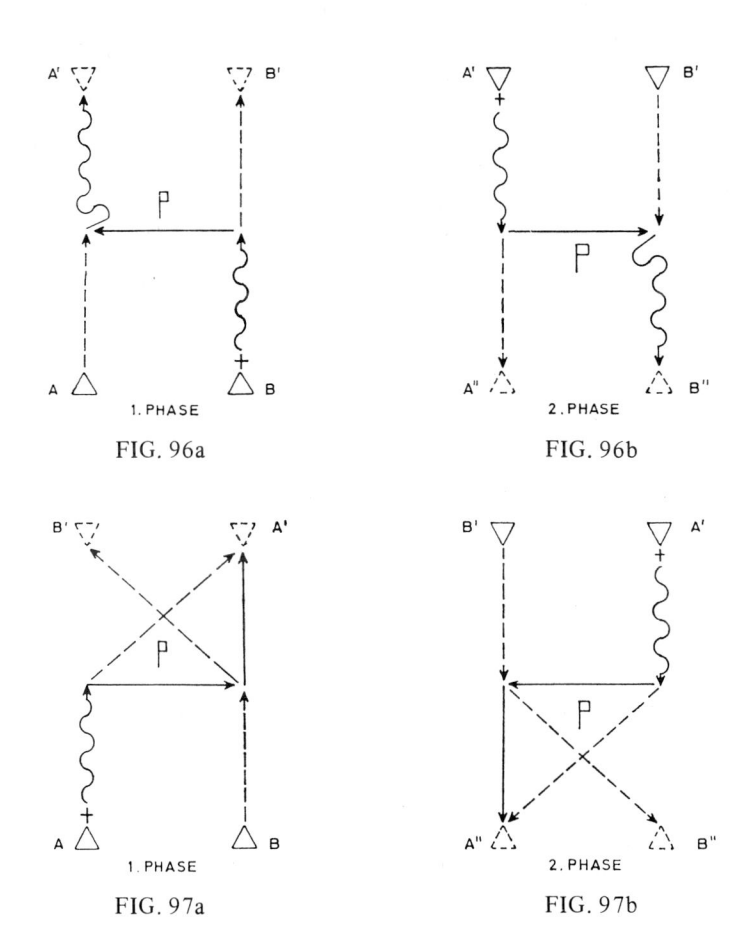

FIG. 96b 2. PHASE

FIG. 97a 1. PHASE

FIG. 97b 2. PHASE

allows the defender any chance at all for a successful intervention, is the wall pass with the players swopping places. When B has received A's square pass on his forehand, he immediately gives a triangular through pass for A to run on to instead of a diagonal pass; A has in the meantime gone over to the right (*Fig. 97*).

When A and B are changing places, care must be taken to see that B always gives way to his partner who is running onto the ball.

b) If player B starts with the ball and player A gives the wall through pass, then the triangle can be practised on the other (i.e. left) side.

c) In place of the flag, a defender, who still remains passive, is bypassed by the triangulation.

d) Triangulation with a change of positions as in a) above. After the players have swopped positions, a square pass is given back to the passer (*Fig. 98*),

FIG. 98a   1. PHASE

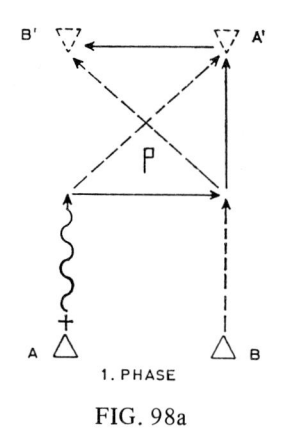

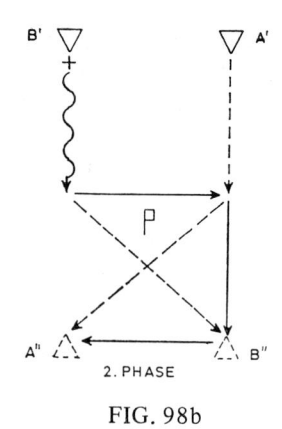

FIG. 98b   2. PHASE

who now dribbles the ball up to the flag (the passive defender), while his partner now takes over the job of giving the wall through pass (second phase). In this exercise therefore triangular passing on the left as well as the right is practised alternately by both players.

4. *Dummy triangulation with change of positions.*
a) After the initial square pass from A to B, B, having controlled the ball with forehand, dummies to give a triangular through pass for A to run onto. While A runs diagonally to the right behind the flag to make himself available for a through pass from B, B, after selling a dummy, runs into A's now vacated position to the left (*Fig. 99*, first phase). On the return run, A and B swop positions (second phase).

Variation: The same exercise with a passive defender.

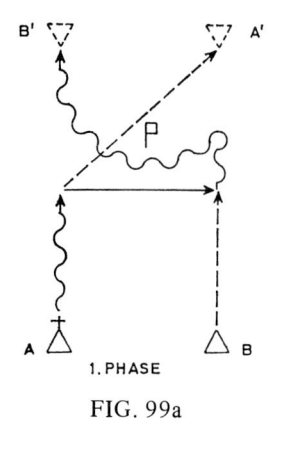

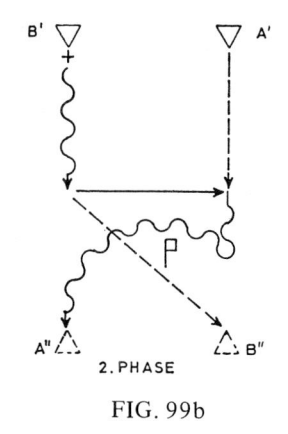

FIG. 99a   1. PHASE

FIG. 99b   2. PHASE

5. *Triangulation with a weak defender*
a) Both forwards should attempt to out-play their opponent with a wall pass in such a way that one of them manages to dribble the ball over the 12m goal-line (*Fig. 100*). To reduce the defender's chances, the pass introducing the triangular movement should be made without any indication of the intention of the ball carrier hard to the other player, outside the defender's reach in the moment the defender tackles the attacker! The condition is imposed on the defender that he must intercept actively 6m away from his goal-line at the latest.

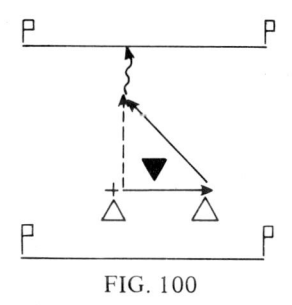

FIG. 100

b) With increasing sureness and confidence the playing area can be reduced.

6. *Triangulation with an active defender in an area of 12 × 12m.*
a) From the three possible methods for by-passing the defender (1, 2a and 3) the method of initiating the triangulation with a pass to the right followed by a diagonal wall pass to the left is the most effective one. As a fourth possibility the forward can also merely dummy to give the square pass, which initiated triangulation, and then run straight on with the ball to the goal-line.

The practice can be said to be successful only when the defender is in a state of constant uncertainty as to which form of triangulation the forwards are going to employ. When all the preparatory exercises (1 to 6) have been coached intensively and frequently enough, the defender will have no chance whatever of counteracting the move.

b) The same on the edge of the circle followed by a shot at goal.

11 The Tactics of Passing

The tactics to be adopted by a team must always proceed from the capabilities of that team as well as from their opponent's style of play. Where possible, therefore, tactics should be planned so as to surprise the other side. Quite independent of team formations or strategies in attack, this principle is also generally valid for tactics in passing.

Even if an individual player succeeds, especially on artificial turf, often in winning a personal duel against a defender, a combined movement between two or more players is the safest and normal procedure to get into the circle and into a position for a shot at goal. In a match, therefore, and for energy saving reasons, passing is more frequently to be used than dribbling. The pass is the 'soul' of hockey and to master it is a prerequisite for carrying out any tactical plan.

In order to ensure successful passing, all players must understand and learn the language of passing and receiving. Before passing the ball the passer should know when, how and where the receiver wishes to pick up the ball. It is absolutely fruitless for the passer to indicate when, how or where the ball will be passed, if the receiver is not ready for the pass. The receiver should make his team-mate pass after establishing with the passer an eye-contact, through body movements and the position of his stick. The majority of the mistakes in passing are caused, apart from lack of skill, because the passer rather than the receiver has instigated the pass (see also page 122).

The higher the level of communication between two players, the more chances exist of retaining possession, of making goal scoring passes and of deceiving the defenders. The fast, mobile and skilful play of the modern defender who allows little space and time to his opponent when marking him closely will be less successful when the players in possession of the ball read each other's game. Once the information has been understood by the ball carrier, he will react accordingly. Provided his technical ability and tactical knowledge is highly developed, he should be able to pass the ball, exactly where the receiver wanted it.

What makes passing even more difficult is the requirement that the player in possession of the ball is disciplined to look for and carry out those passes demanded by the team tactics. He generally should prefer to pass instead of attempting to beat his opponent especially when his aim is

— to 'pass by' an opponent = attacking pass

- to allow a better positioned team-mate to attack with less risk = movement pass
- to relieve pressure from his own defence (clearance to a front runner) = attacking pass
- to initiate an attacking move = attacking pass
- to retain possession (with a back pass) = possession pass

A good pass is characterised – by its necessity (very often players pass the ball when there is absolutely no reason for passing) – by its accuracy – by the exactness of the timing – by the speed and by the disguise of direction.

The team whose players do not possess these abilities (which can be remarkably improved by intensive coaching) will hardly meet with success, however much stickwork and dribbling ability their players do have. Poor passing is a failing which cannot be offset by other abilities.

Accuracy in direction

Accuracy in passing is without doubt one of a side's most powerful weapons for overcoming an opponent. It depends not only on the technical ability of the passer but, to a special degree, on the skilful movement into position of the receiver who should instigate the pass instead of reacting to it!

The short pass is the easiest, for the shorter the distance the ball has to travel, the less the danger that a ball will not reach the receiver. A player who cannot pass accurately over 10m will most certainly not be able to do so over thirty. To hit a long pass is a very difficult manoeuvre, yet when it is used accurately and at the right moment, it is also the most effective. The times when defenders used to clear their lines by long, hard hits upfield are well past. In fact, there is little sense in simply hitting the ball as far upfield as possible. The ball will more easily fall into the possession of the opponents, who can then immediately mount a new attack. The modern defender clears up the situation, and at the same time, initiates an attack. To do this, he does not always use the long pass, but, more frequently, a short one. But his job is not finished with the clearance pass alone. The defender must immediately run into position again to make himself available for a return pass. The short pass, reaching only the nearest player, must also be part of the modern defender's stock-in-trade.

In a match, passes are made in all directions, to the front (through passes), to the side (square or diagonal passes) and backwards (back passes). The tactical aim in passing is to keep the ball in one's own team, so it means that every pass which is intercepted by the other side not only gives away the chance of a shot at goal but it also nullifies all the efforts of the individual player and of his team.

In order to be able to give an accurate pass, the passer must have checked up previously on the position of his team-mates in relation to himself. The position of the receiver's stick, his disposition and tenseness in the various muscle groups, all serve as important indicators to the passer regarding the direction, timing and speed of the pass. For example, if the inside left is waiting in the side-on position, for a pass from the centre half, with his right shoulder pointing towards the passer, the latter should always pass the ball to the inside left on his reverse-stick side and not at his heels or even behind his back. In the same way, the inside right, with his left shoulder towards the passer, should always receive the ball on his right with the forehand. If, however, the ball arrives further off, behind his back, the inside right may obstruct when receiving the ball. In all these cases the following holds good: the passer must always play the ball to the side indicated by the receiver (see exercise 3 in 'The hit' page 48). The shorter the distance of the pass is, the more accurate its direction must be, for a long pass gives the receiver more time to get into position, even if the direction of the pass is inaccurate. However, in that case the opponent also has more time to intercept the ball.

A common mistake is lack of responsibility when passing. Players often hit the ball in any direction without looking first, only then to realise that the player for whom the pass was intended has no chance of reaching the ball. *Before* the pass takes place, both players must make certain that no opponent is standing along the line of the pass, that no opponent can reach the line of the pass in time to intercept it and that no opponent can tackle the player receiving the ball from behind. These conditions must be observed all the more, the longer the pass is. The direction of the pass is determined by the position of its target. A colleague's stick is not always the target, however: the ball is often played through the gap between two players or between an opponent and the side-line. In these cases, the exact direction of the pass is determined by the size of the gap, the speed of the player to run onto the pass and the ground conditions. The larger the gap, the more possibilities there are for the accuracy of the pass. If the gap is very small, then the ball has to be flicked low along a clearly defined line or else it will be intercepted. If the gap is so small that the reach of one opponent on the open side and of a second opponent on his reverse stick can close it, then a pass in that direction along the ground is no longer possible.

The timing of the pass

The best moment to give a pass is when the opponent makes his attempt to tackle the player in possession. Naturally the moment for giving the pass will be determined not only by the conduct of one's opponent but also by the build-up of one's own team attack. Every good player should learn to feel (with the help of numerous little games 2:1, 3:2 and 4:3) when the precise moment arrives to pass the ball!

The pass should take place at the moment that the receiver is ready to run to it and is not yet in an off-side position.

The speed (force) of the pass

The speed of the pass is decisive for the swift flow in combined movements. The players must have fixed in their minds the need to lose as little time as possible in passing. Each pass must have a definite speed. Any substantial variation in that necessary speed may well result in the ball being lost. The ball should reach the gap between the two players in the shortest space of time but taking into consideration the individual ability of the player receiving the ball. The mistake is frequently made of hitting short passes too weakly. Slow passing allows the opponents time to run into the line of the pass to intercept. If, for example, a player, after a brief look around, sees a colleague standing unmarked fifteen metres away, he must count on the fact, in modern hockey, that the covering defender is lying in wait in the immediate vicinity of the other player, probably just behind him. If the ball arrives very slowly, this generally gives the opponent sufficient time to run forward and reach the ball first. This example shows very clearly how important it is to run to meet an approaching ball. If the pass, and with it a combined move, is to proceed smoothly, then no players can afford to wait passively for the ball to come to them (see 'Tactical considerations before or whilst taking the ball' page 35).

Passing reaches its highest tempo when players pass first time to each other, from which very rapid combined play results. However the first time pass is not always possible, so the ball has to be stopped for a short while before the pass can be given. The player who wants to be able to move the ball quickly, at least at certain stages of the game, must understand quite clearly that the fastest dribbler can never compare with the speed of a ball when hit.

Disguising the direction of the pass

The player must learn to disguise the direction of his pass (*Fig. 13*) but to avoid misunderstandings, he must practise so thoroughly together with his team-mates that they get to know the characteristics of the passer.

The direction of the pass can be disguised, when for instance the player does not look in the direction in which he intends to play the ball or if the player does not dribble the ball in the direction in which he is going finally to

pass but adopts a totally different path. Further methods of disguising the direction of the pass, are
a) a stick dummy executed at the same time as a body swerve (see page 132).
b) picking the stick up as if to hit, and then dribbling the ball on (see page 90, exercise 5) or using a different technique for the pass (i.e. a flick).
c) a disguised pass (hit, push or flick) (see pp. 61-64).

All actions occurring in the game, including dummy manoeuvres, must be practised so thoroughly that they can stem almost automatically from the course of the game.

If the principles outlined above are heeded when passing, then the ball will certainly reach the player to whom it is destined.

12 The Defence - How to Improve it Individually and Collectively

Defence is the job of all the players, also of the forwards, who must frequently play their part in defence. Their primary defensive task should always be to hinder the opposing defence in building up new attacks smoothly. A forward who fails to do this and who does not tackle back after losing the ball or after a shot at goal, is tactically immature.

In contrast to the forwards, the most important task of the defenders is to prevent goals from being scored by the opposition. The main difference in difficulty between attacking and defensive play lies in the fact that a player, when attacking, can usually determine his own moves, whereas the defender has to adapt his to the opposing forward and react correspondingly to his movements and actions. The speed of the game indoors and on artificial turf demands often that the defender especially in the mid-field reacts to a situation rather than creates a situation which is to his advantage as was often seen on natural grass.

But to be able to react correspondingly on any surface good footwork is a necessity. The defender must like a boxer be on his toes (not flat footed) and well-balanced, in order to shift his weight rapidly. Correctly timed defensive actions, such as jabs or lunges towards the ball, in any direction, forwards, sideways and even more quickly backwards, are then much easier to produce. Apart from a certain mobility and dexterity, the defender requires, above all, the ability to size up the overall situation and rapid powers of decision. When the opposing side is in possession, a well trained defender will always keep a close eye on the ball, his opponent, and the overall situation, so as to be able to tackle at the correct moment, to intercept a pass or be able to prevent his opponent from running into an open space. The ability to decide speedily for the appropriate move to be carried out, depends, to a great extent, on the player's capacity to grasp the situation.

A sound defence is an important factor for morale, especially when a team is playing away or against very strong opposition. The feeling of safety and confidence in the team's defence benefits the forward's play and gives them fresh encouragement.

Psychological reasons speak in favour of the defender taking good care to see that his first contact with the ball is as successful as possible. That gives him great personal self-confidence. If, at the first encounter, the defender meets his man in a hard and determined way, the attacker at the next encounter will, under certain circumstances, be already a little inhibited and the prospects of success for the defender will be substantially increased.

A successful defensive play, which imbues the side with encouragement and self-confidence, is dependent as much on the performance of individual players as on co-operation between all the members of the side. Without mutual support and assistance no defence today can expect success.* Before the members of the defence learn how to support each other (see pp. 143-145), they must first achieve mastery over the individual principles of defence.

The ten most important factors which determine the method of tackling.

The method of tackling depends on:
1. The position of the tackler in relation to that of his team-mates.
2. The position of the tackler in relation to the attacker or attackers.
3. The position of the tackler in the field, taking especially into account the lines of the field (22.90m line!)
4. The way the attacker dribbles the ball.
5. The habits, the ability and the characteristics of the attacker.
6. The fact whether the ball is stationary or not.
7. The ground conditions.
8. The interpretations of the umpire.
9. The ability and psycho-motor qualities of the tackler.
10. The tackles carried out before.

The ten most important general rules for tackling individually with success

1. Do not run towards the opponent in possession of the ball when the ball is well controlled.
2. Use the most of the surface of your stick for the tackle.
3. Watch the ball and have less attention for the body and stick positioning of the attacker.
4. Slow down the attack in order to gain time and support.
5. When possible create the situation which suits you best instead of reacting only.
6. Select the correct line of approach.
7. Execute dummy moves.
8. Force the attacker in possession of the ball to act predictably.
9. Vary your methods of tackling and do not prefer the same tackles all the time.

---

* see in 'The Advanced Science of Hockey' — 'The development from zonal and man-to-man marking to combined marking'.

10. Be ready to attack after a successful tackle.

Psycho-motor qualities for tackling individually with success

1. Quick reaction (eye).
2. Speed of movement (optimal co-operation between muscle and nerves) guarantees suprise in your tackling.
3. Optical-physical assessment, which quality depends on concentration, vision, experience, knowledge, patience and quick processing of information.
4. Dexterity and balance.

Positional play

In principle, the defender should stand between his opponent and his own goal on an imaginary straight line running from the attacker to the middle of his goal (*Fig. 101*).

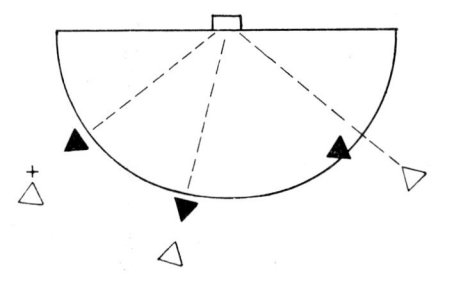

FIG. 101

He can, in certain situations, deviate from this theoretical line, when, for example, the ball is on the opposite side of the field. Then the defender should move a little away from the imaginary line, towards the middle in the direction of the ball (*Fig. 101*). Such a change of position makes it possible for the defender, who has moved inwards, to be able to assist his colleague more quickly and more easily if he is beaten. Since the defender, however, has always sufficient time, if there is a pass to the right, to cover the opponent entrusted to his charge, this change in position represents no risk at all.

One cannot make a generally valid statement as to the distance to be left between the defender and the forward being marked. That depends on several factors:
1. On the speed of the opposing forward and on the speed of the defender. If the defender is faster than the forward, he can stand quite close to

him. A slower defender, however, should place himself three to four metres away from the forward.
2. On the technical ability of the opponent. The higher the technical level of the attacker, the closer the defender should stay to him in order to intercept the pass to him or worry him when receiving the ball.
3. On the player's position on the pitch. If the attacker is a long way away from his opponent's goal, the defender may without any problem be metres away from him. But the closer the forward comes to goal, the more dangerous he is and the more closely he must be marked.

A very important condition in positional play is that the defender should keep his opponent constantly in front of him and yet, at the same time, keep an eye on the ball. This two-fold task can only be avoided if the defender has learnt how to look both directly and out of the corner of his eye (peripheral vision). Correct positioning is, of course, a most important aspect of defence but is not sufficient in itself to repulse the opponents' assault.

Methods of tackling

1. **Lunging to tackle (sweep tackle)**
Lunging to challenge is the commonest form of tackling, and is particularly successful if the opponent does not have the ball fully under his control − for instance if he has let the ball roll too far away from his stick whilst dribbling.

The lunge should start from the 'basic defensive position' in which the

Fig. 102. Miguel de Paz (Spain) lunging forward to tackle.

stick is held in both hands with the head of the stick pointing into the ground. Lowering the point of gravity, dancing on the toes whilst keeping the weight equally distributed on both feet, enabling the defender to make quick defensive reactions in any required direction. As the lunge tackle is off the left foot, the left hand flings the stick (until then held in both hands) powerfully towards the ball (*Fig. 102*). By putting his left foot forward, the defender can increase his reach; another benefit of reaching quickly out as far as possible is that if the first lunge tackle should fail, the tackler may try again by stepping back with his left foot: he will not have to turn round, if his reaction to failure the first time is quick enough. If the lunge is made off the right foot, which the game situation sometimes demands, (or if the player fails to let go of the stick with his right hand whilst lunging), then not only is his reach impaired, but his view of play is restricted, since his upper torso is necessarily bent forward more than if the lunge were off the left foot. This restricted vision can easily lead to collisions with other players. In contrast to the left shoulder, the right (together with the free right hand) should generally be kept well away from the ball (see *Fig. 102*).

Methodical series of drills for coaching the lunge tackle.
1. *Lunge tackle without a partner.*
Players individually practise the defensive lunge off the left foot, at a ball lying about two metres in front of them. They should practise both starting from the basic position, and after 'dancing on their toes'.
2. *Lunge tackle with a partner.*
Two players stand facing each other about five metres apart, and lunge towards each other simultaneously, in order to test each other's reach: the ball remains motionless between them. Watch for technical accuracy in carrying out the lunge tackle.
3. *Lunge tackle with a partner; competitive practice.*
On a signal from the coach, two players both lunge-tackle at the ball placed midway between them. The aim is to touch the ball first. If the right hand keeps hold of the stick, then an otherwise-successful attempt should not count. The winner should be the first to five. In order to make the lunge as quickly as possible, the player should fling his stick immediately towards the ball, without a preparatory 'winding up'.

Variation: each player should try to take the ball past the opponent after having touched it first.
4. *Lunge with a stationary partner who moves the ball in the moment of the tackle.*
Each defender has to try to touch his partner's ball with his stick. The quicker his stick moves towards the ball, the greater the percentage of success. When

the player with the ball manages to anticipate the moment of tackling, the defender should carry out dummy moves. How many tackles does the defender need to touch the ball?

5. *Defending against a passive forward dribbling the ball.*

In order to avoid injuries due to lunge tackles hitting the shins and feet, forwards should dribble the ball straight in front of the body, close to the stick. When the forward comes within reach of the tackler, the latter lunges forward from a position a little to the left of his opponent, rather than from immediately in front. Such a side-on position increases the arc through which the tackler has opportunities to gain possession of the ball. If the tackler succeeds, then he should transfer all his weight onto his left foot and try to bring the deflected ball under control within a few paces. If he fails in the tackle, he should retract his front foot, in order to have a second chance to gain possession.

6. *As in 5., but lunging with the reverse stick.*
7. *As in 5., but with or without preceding feints, lunging with forehand or reverse stick.*
8. *As in 5., but with a delayed tackle.*

The defender lets the opponent almost run past him and tackles with the full length of the stick in a very low body position (*Fig. 103*), when the forward's ball is level with him. Active dribbling by the forward, with sudden changes of direction, is not allowed, since his role is passive. He should always control the ball close to the curve of the stick.

9. *Lunge tackle as a competition.*

Any number of players dribble a ball inside a limited area. Each player has to try to move the balls of other players out of the playing area, using lunge tackles, without losing control of his own ball. The last player still dribbling his own ball is the winner. If a player loses his ball, he goes into an adjoining area where a separate competition is held for those knocked out of the first.

10. *Lunge tackle with the right hand only*

In case there is no time for turning towards the right, the defender may change the position of his hands and lunges forward with only his right hand on the top of the stick.

2. Tackling in retreat

The lunge tackle should be used by a defender especially when the attacker has allowed the ball to roll too far away from his stick whilst dribbling. If the forward has full control of his ball, this type of tackle is less recommended: because a well trained forward with very good vision would have little difficulty in avoiding the tackle by taking the ball out of his reach.

In tackling in retreat, the defender moves out of the forward's path to place himself at his side, thus presenting him with an open space. The players do not immediately confront each other, therefore, but run side by side. The defender continues to shadow the forward thus, until he sees a favourable opportunity for dispossessing him.

The intelligent defender tries to create suitable situations for a successful tackle as he follows the forward back by means of dummy movements with his stick and body (e.g. by pretending to lunge forwards). By these means he forces his opponent into making involuntary moves, so that the defender's chances of success in the duel between the two increases. The great advantage of tackling in retreat is that the marker, after an unsuccessful attempt to tackle, has one, two, or more further chances, as the forward has not already beaten him. But if, on the other hand, the defender lunges forward to tackle from a stationary, frontal position and fails to win the ball, he has then, first of all, to transfer back his weight, which is now well forward, turn round and then start running after a standing start. After all this the forward will be well away.

It is important while tackling in retreat for the defender always to keep his eye on the ball. If he observes this advice, he will never be deceived by a stick dummy or a body swerve into making a false move himself.

When tackling in retreat from the right, the defender moves slightly out to the path of the dribble to the left and turns in order to shadow at the right shoulder of the attacker and block the attacker's possible pass to the right. When tackling in retreat from the left (see *Fig. 104*) the hook of the stick faces down so that the flat face can play the ball out.

Fig. 103. Perfect reverse-stick tackling by A. Chesney of New Zealand, against Mahendran of Malaysia (Third World Cup)

Methodical series of drills for tackling in retreat.

1. *Preliminary exercise (shadow running).*
Two players run without sticks, slowly at first, but later rather more quickly, maintaining a distance of 2m between them. Whereas A runs forwards, sideways or backwards at will in an effort to surprise the other player, B has to imitate all these movements in such a way that he constantly maintains the required 2m distance from his partner.

2. *Shadowing by the defender.*
a) The attacker, playing between the 22.90m line and the goal line without a stick, tries out various individual attacking movements at moderate speed (dodging, body swerve and abrupt changes of speed) to try and beat the defender, who meets him face to face but then keeps to his side, to the goal line.

It is the defender's task at this stage on the practice to adopt the correct positioning (see 'Positional play', page 127) relative to his opponent and prevent his running into the open space. The defender must not actually touch his opponent.

b) As in a) above except that both players now carry their sticks but still without a ball.

c) The practice is further extended in that the attacker is now given a ball but the defender is still not allowed actually to take it away from him, but should, constantly maintain his correct position in relation to the ball and his opponent. In exercises b) above and c) the defender should quite intentionally put into effect various defensive dodges to upset the approaching forward. This exercise can be made competitive by seeing who can delay for the longest time a successful attack by an opposing forward.

3. *Tackling in retreat.*
Two players stand opposite each other about 6m apart. There is a ball midway between them, and a cone 6-8m behind each player. After lunging towards the ball, each player transfers his weight back to the right foot, turns to the right, and tries to be first to touch his cone with his stick. At first this exercise should be done only making a right-hand turn (i.e. simulating tackling in retreat on the open side). Putting too much weight on the front foot in making the lunge tackle will slow down any backward turn in the direction of the cone. Each player should therefore try to push off from his left leg while it is still bent as he turns: this requires that when he touches the ball, his centre of gravity is not quite over the left leg. When he is running back to the cone, he should hold the stick only in his left hand.

When he is tackling in retreat using a reverse-stick lunge, the defender needs to alter his positioning. Now he has the attacker on his left side, with his own right foot forward. He should hold the stick well in front of his right hip so as to block the forward's path and force the forward to go to his left (reverse-stick) side (see *Fig. 103*).

4. *Tackling in retreat against a forward dribbling passively.*
The defender waits for the forward to come towards him, and then moves to one side of the forward's path, letting the forward come level with him on either the open or reverse side. He then shadows the attacker in retreat, after feinting a lunge tackle. As he shadows, he makes further dummy movements with both stick and body. As the defender improves, the passive attacker should increase the speed at which he dribbles.

5. *Active defence in a square (15 × 15m square), against active forwards.*
Five forwards, one after the other, attempt to beat the active defender who tackles in retreat within the square (but who remains in the square the whole time) in such a way that they can dribble the ball across the end line. If the ball goes out of play over a side-line or over the other end of the square, or if the defender can dispossess the forward without fouling, then the defender scores one point. If the defender fouls, then the forward has another turn. Each forward has two attempts against the defender. After ten attacks the defender swops places with one of the forwards. Who is the most successful defender?
Variation: the forwards come from different directions and try to run with the ball through the defended square.

6. *Tackling in retreat with active defence.*
Playing between the 22.90m line and the goal line, the defender now attempts to dispossess the attacker, who constantly alters the direction of his dribbling. If the dribbler succeeds in beating the defender with the ball, and in reaching the goal line before him, the attacker scores one point, just as the defender does, if he succeeds in winning the ball. After each attempt the positions are reversed. The condition is imposed on the defender at each attempt to tackle that he has to retreat for at least 10m before the real attempt to tackle is made (*Fig. 104*).

7. *One against one on a pitch 22.90m long, with goals 10m wide.*
The two players engage each other until one is able to dribble the ball over his opponent's goal line.
After a goal is scored or if the ball goes over the goal line, the two players

Fig. 104. Paul Svehlik of England about to tackle Laeeq of Pakistan

take a rest. While two reserve players, who have been spectators behind the two goals, carry on with the game, the two players resting go behind the goals, ready to take over again the next time a goal is scored or the ball goes off over the goal line. The new attack is always started from the end at which the last goal was scored or at which the ball went out of play. Thus the opponent of the man in possession is automatically the defender.

Apart from lunging, blocking, jabbing and tackling in retreat, following the game situation, which few players in the world master, the players can learn two important tactical lessons when the ball is lost: immediate pursuit of the opponent and the lightning-fast switch from defence to attack.

3. **The block tackle** (*Fig. 105*)

4. **The jab*** (*Fig. 64*) (see '*The Advanced Science of Hockey*', 2nd ed)

Worrying the opponent when receiving the ball

Worrying an opponent when receiving the ball is easiest to do when remaining within the opponent's reach. The skilful defender can work out the likely direction of a pass from the body movements, head and eye movements, and the characteristics of the player in possession of the ball. If the defender is unable to intercept the ball by running quickly onto the line of the pass,

---

* The first five exercises for lunge tackling could also be used to practise the jab.

Fig. 105. A Russian defender blocks successfully Hazelhurst (Australia) with the stick horizontally placed on the ground.

he should at least attempt to take the forward by surprise from behind at the moment that he is bringing the ball under control, so as to make the forward obstruct. This frequently occurs in a match, because, in such cases the forward is directing all his attention to the approaching ball and forgets, often to adopt a side-on position to the ball, and, more important, to run and meet the pass.

*Methodical series of drills for worrying the opponent when receiving the ball**

1. A player passes the ball from a distance of 22.90m to his partner standing opposite, behind whom stands the defender. The defender attempts to pick up the ball before the proper receiver by running round him and then giving it back to the original passer. The ball should be passed unexpectedly without any obvious preparation. At first the attacker is to move only 1m and later on 2m towards the ball.
2. The practice is made more difficult; the attacker now hinders the defender as he runs forward by moving towards the ball himself in a side-on position. Both the defender and the forward now try to reach the approaching ball first. Whoever can return the ball to the passer without fouling, is the winner. Whilst the two players are fighting for possession of the ball, the passer should move into a new position.

---

*see also 'Tactical considerations before or whilst receiving the ball' pp. 35-37.

3. Finally, the defender is instructed not to take the ball away from the forward until the moment that the forward is trying to control the ball. In this case when the ball is for 1/10 second stationary the jab (see *Fig. 64*) is the most effective and surprising way of gaining possession of the ball.

Close marking an opponent

If the defender follows his opponent everywhere he goes, we then talk of marking him out of the game or closemarking. The defender directs his attention to his opponent as well as to the ball, without, however, losing sight of the overall situation.

Close marking an opponent demands that the defender be in peak condition for he has to keep up with his opponent whenever he moves into an open space. Good footwork and balance are prerequisites for being able to mark an opponent this closely at all times. However, if the opponent is superior to the defender in speed, stamina and agility and especially when he has a very good understanding with the ball carrier, then obviously the attempts at marking him will be unsuccessful. Close marking is best practised by simple games involving running and frequent sudden stops and unexpected changes of direction (see 'Developing flexibility and dexterity', page 186). Training defenders to mark opponents out under match conditions is best undertaken in small games with forwards attacking large or small goals (three against three, four against four or five against five).

Learning how to mark a man is very important for developing an individual grounding in defence and it forms the basis for all other types of marking. As the principles of individual defensive play are learned earlier in this way than, for example, in learning the zonal marking, close marking should be learned first and practised for a long time before moving on to other aspects of marking. Once the players have learned how to mark their man, they will understand much more easily about covering or combined marking (covering the gap and marking the man). If, on the contrary, covering is introduced first, as used to be the case, then learning to mark a man will entail later difficulty.*

If a defender tries to mark a dangerous forward out of the game, he is in no way playing purely defensively. Rather, his marking is designed to aid the attack, reinforcing the need for attacking tactics, because the man in possession is immediately tackled. The defender should never look on passively when his man goes into the thick of the game. Modern defenders, who mark

---

* see *'The Advanced Science of Hockey'* — 'The importance of man-to-man marking in children's hockey'.

their man tightly and very early, are not playing defensively but are attacking as soon as an opportunity arises to join the attack.

Graduated series of small games designed to gain experience in close marking

1.
a) *One against one with a neutral passer (Fig. 106)*
    A mid-field player (link-man) pushes the ball over at least 10m to his forward who is to try and score a goal while being tightly marked by a defender. The free hit must be taken within five seconds. In this period of time, the forward must have taken a visual agreement with the passer and must have got away from his defender, so that he can receive the ball without obstructing. For each goal scored by the forward without obstruction, the forward and the passer receive one point.

    The players change round after ten attacks. The defender becomes the forward, the forward becomes the passer and he takes on the defender's position. Who has scored the most points after the thirty attacks?

    FIG. 106

b) *One against one with a neutral passer (variation).*
    If the defender wins the ball and has succeeded in passing to the passer, he changes over to the attack and the former forward takes over the defence. Whoever manages to score a goal, can carry on in attack. The passer is not allowed to score.

    In these and the following exercises, the defender can practise and will improve: marking a forward closely, accurate passing after a successful tackle (while still under pressure from an opponent), the quick changeover from defence to attack and also worrying the opponent when receiving the ball and tackling in retreat, after failing to anticipate the pass to the forward.

The effect of these practices on the forward will be to establish eye contact with the passer for the moment and the direction of the pass, the ball without obstructing receive, then move the defender and beat him with carrying out dummy moves.

The passer learns the correct moment for giving a pass and how to agree certain movements with his forward which must be carried out without misunderstanding.

2.
a) *Two against two with a neutral passer (as in 1. a) and 1. b) above).*
b) *Variation:*
Line-up as in 1. a) above. This time, however, the passer must pass the ball while on the run over at least 10m, immediately after a slalom round three flags, to one of the two forwards who have become available for a second. While dribbling, the passer must look up from the ball, so as to read from the 'cues' of his team-mates where and when to pass.
c) *Two against two with a neutral passer and sweeper.*
The passer, from a stationary position, serves one of the forwards who has become available and who, with the assistance of the passer and the second forward, has to try and score a goal against the two defenders who are marking and the one sweeper who is covering. The passer, however, may not score a goal and should always maintain a distance of 8-10m from his forwards. The sweeper behind the defenders cuts off passes from the passer into the gaps and always helps out when one of the defenders is beaten by a forward.

3.
a) *Three against three with a neutral passer and sweeper in front of the circle.*
Line-up as in 2. c) above except that there is now one extra player, both in attack and defence. By means of frequent interchanging of positions, the three forwards should try to make close-marking more difficult for the defenders. The defenders should apply close or combined marking.
b) *Four against four, dribbling the ball over the line.*
On losing the ball, three players in the team concentrate on marking their opposite numbers, whereas the fourth acts as sweeper. The side in possession plays with three forwards and one passer, who becomes the sweeper when the ball is lost. Passer and sweeper may not dribble into the opposing half. The game takes place across the width of the field.
c) *Four (three) against four (three) on one goal, with a goal-keeper.*
Only after at least one pass amongst the players of one side can a goal be scored.

4.
a) *Four against four with a passer and sweeper in front of the circle (as in 3. a).*
b) *Five against five, dribbling the ball over the line.*
Four players in the team, losing the ball, must concentrate on marking their opposite numbers, using close or combined markings (as in 3. b).
c) *Four against four, with two mid-field players, one sweeper and one goalkeeper.*
Neither mid-field player is allowed to move upfield beyond the 22.90m line. They can play the ball to each other until one of the four forwards being tightly marked by the opposition has been able to break free, in order to receive a pass over at least 10m.
d) *Variation on c).* One of the mid-field players may now, occasionally, join in with the attack. By doing this the sweeper is forced to take on the extra man. As the defence is no longer superior in numbers, the remaining defenders cannot continue with their close marking. The change to covering, whereby the defender furthest away from the ball has to cover and the defender positioned closest to the 'tackler' takes on the role of backing him up. The second mid-field player, as previously, should not cross the 22.90m line. The mid-field players are not allowed to pass the ball more than three times amongst themselves.
e) *Variation on c).* If the defence can get the ball into their possession and pass three times among themselves, they score one point; so, too, do the forwards if they can touch the ball within the circle. A goal scored counts two points.
f) *Variation on c).* Counter attacking allowed.
If a defender gains possession of the ball, they attempt to pass it as quickly as possible through one of two goals, 4m wide, placed on the centre-line in the left wing and right wing positions. Immediately after losing the ball the attacking side must quickly change over to defence, with the four forwards marking their respective defenders, and the two mid-field players guarding the two goals on the centre-line. The team which first scores twenty points wins (see 4. e).

These methodical practice games guarantee the step by step development of close marking from the individual, through the group to the whole team; they guarantee also that defensive technique and tactics are trained both individually and collectively. From one type of game to the next, the players practising become more capable in summing up in a flash the state of play, of anticipating the most appropriate solution and then carrying it out automatically, whilst the ever-changing situation puts new demands on their tactical thoughts and actions. Apart from considering the position of team-mates, a watch must be kept on the positions, actions and probable intentions of the opponents; above all, the ball must constantly be watched.

Finally, attention must be directed to the fact that sufficient time has to be spent on these drills in training and that, in one week, only one of the 15 various types of game should be introduced for, otherwise, the introduction of close marking in a game could be a failure.

For more details about marking and covering see pp. 143-145.

Extending the defender's reach

A good defender is able to use his reach to its best advantage. To control as large an area of the pitch as possible, the player's reach must be improved and extended by training.

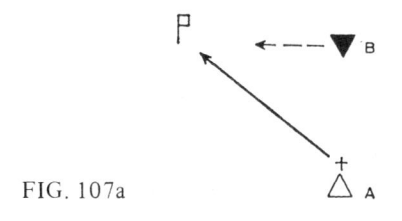

FIG. 107a

Fig. 107b. Poor use of reach by a defender for not letting his left hand go

Methodical drills for extending the player's reach.
1. Player A faces player B at a distance of 4m (*Fig. 107a*). To the right of player B, and level with him, is a flag (3m away). When A plays the ball in the direction of the flag, B alters his basic stance by executing a quarter turns to the right towards the ball on the right foot, and, at the same time, places the left well past the right foot. At the end of this sideways lunge, after transferring the outside leg, both feet point towards the flag or towards the ball. The stick is then held with the left hand only, and the right hand is released. Only by leaving hold of the stick with the right hand, can the right shoulder be held back, thereby allowing the left shoulder to be pushed further forward towards the ball.
  Variation: Lack of time may force the defender to neglect that the outside leg should be transferred across. Instead the defender widens the distance between both feet and reaches out only with the right hand gripping the stick at the top of the handle (see *Fig. 1a*).
2. When extending the player's reach on the reverse stick side (*Fig. 108*), the right foot is transferred past the other to the left, at the same time as the player makes a quarter turn towards the left on the left foot, so that, at the moment of stopping the ball with the reverse stick, both feet are pointing in the direction of the ball.

   Since the right foot at the moment of stopping is in front of the left, it follows that the left shoulder, in relation to the right, is pushed forwards only slightly. After the reverse-stick stop, which can be carried out in various ways (see 'The Reverse stick stop' page 29), attention must be paid to see that the back of the left hand points backwards. In contrast to the grip from underneath, with the back of the hand pointing downwards, this grip enables a greater degree of power to be developed.

   The practices outlined in 1 and 2 above are best carried out in front of a wall or a fence.
   Variation: The defender because of lack of time does not move his right leg across and moves out only with the left hand on the top of the stick (see *Fig. 109b*).
3. Players A, B and C form an equilateral triangle, the sides of which are

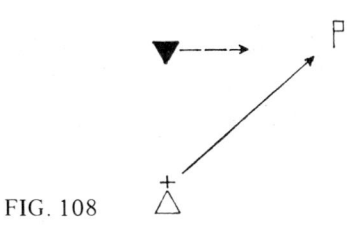

FIG. 108

6m long. Between B and C, who stand in front of a flag, a defender places himself facing the passer, player A (*Fig. 109a*). The latter is given a ball and plays it alternately, first to B and then to C, without, in so doing, leaving the triangle. The defender's task is to extend his reach, dependent on the time available with or without transferring the outside leg and intercepting the pass to B or C with one or two hands on the stick. After every ten passes from the player in position A, the players change round in a clockwise direction, that is to say, B takes A's place and C moves into the triangle to become the defender. Only when the use of a player's reach has been mastered, both to the left and to the right, by all four players, may the passer send the ball in any sequence he cares, to left or to right. After ten passes which defender has picked up the most?

4. The practice described in 3 above can be increased in intensity by doing away with players B and C. The defender now stands in the middle of a goal and, by use of his reach, must prevent passes from player A going

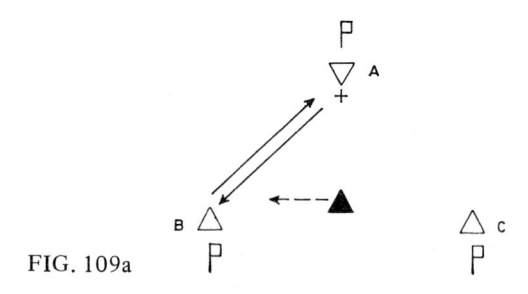

FIG. 109a

Fig.109b. With a block tackle P. Trump (West Germany) makes maximum use of his stick placing his reverse stick horizontally on the ground. Because of the position of his team-mate on his left and because of lack of time he has decided not to transfer his outside leg across.

through the goal. The defender is allowed to extend his reach slightly by taking a short preliminary step with the nearest leg towards the ball reaching out.

Who scores the most goals with pushed passes? This, too, is best practised in front of a wall or fence, so that fetching balls that are missed does not take too much time.

Covering in defence

Winning a game cannot be achieved by attacking only. So in addition to developing the individual defensive skills, the necessity of teaching a combined pattern of defence in order to prevent goals being scored, becomes obvious.

In the collective defence a player independent of the instructions he has received should always attempt to position himself in such a way that he can fulfil the two most important but conflicting tasks: marking an opponent and at the same time covering the space behind or beside him.

Since generations of defenders used exclusively the zonal marking allowing the opponents the space and the time to bring the ball under control but as the disadvantages of granting the attack sufficient time to control the ball and to assess a variety of attacking plays were systematically exploited by the ever growing technical and tactical expertise of the attackers, the need for change became evident. First, the increased number of defenders narrowed the space for which each player was responsible. Then the man-to-man marking with the use of a sweeper became the most effective pattern in the collective defence and finally a combination between zonal and man-to-man marking in which the two important duties of marking an opponent and covering space could be fulfilled with less conflicts at the same time (especially through the co-operation with the covering free man in defence), was considered to be best suited to consolidate the weak defence (see in '*The Advanced Science of Hockey*', chapter 'The development from zonal and man-to-man marking to combined marking).

A defence, in which the individual players co-operate well, knows how to lend mutual support, quickly and efficiently, when the opponents have beaten one of its own men. Changing positions is an extremely important weapon in defence and it takes place whenever a forward breaks through and is taken on by the player nearest to the beaten defender. The swop in position must be carried out very carefully and prudently. A few examples will show how this swopping of positions in defence must be carried out, first with the orthodox line-up of five forwards, three halves and two backs.

The right wing has beaten the left half and is approaching the opposing

22.90m line. What must now be done? So that the attack can be checked, the left back, who is nearest to the LH, leaves his own inside forward and slowly approaches the RW. In doing this he pays close attention to see that the winger does not give a through or square pass for his IR to run onto. He must attempt to induce the winger, either to engage in time consuming dribbling, or to make an attempt to beat him. If the winger dribbles this allows the beaten LH time to take over the marking of the inside forward, who has been left by the LB. The numerical balance is therefore once again restored.

Above all, defenders should guard against leaving their own man too early when swopping positions. If the LB leaves his inside forward immediately to take on the RW as he breaks through, he then runs the risk that the RW will pass the ball immediately to the IR, before the LH has been able to take over marking the IR.

If, for example, the opposition centre forward breaks through, then the nearest of the two backs (generally the left back, who can play the ball with forehand) must take on the CF, because he constitutes the greatest danger for the defence. In this case, changing positions is carried out without any great difficulty, since the distance from defender to defender and also between the forwards is much less just in front of the goal than it is in mid-field.

In coaching how to change positions, the coach should constantly watch out to see that there is always a diagonal line-up in defence (*Fig. 129*). The aim of the diagonal line-up is to facilitate the changing of positions in case the opposition breaks through. As the coach is unable to keep on giving instructions during the course of the game from off the pitch, he should designate a player (preferably the CH or GK), who can pass on instructions about correct positional play and about changing positions in this case.

Assistance in defence, by means of interchange of positions among defenders, is made easier if a free man (sweeper) is employed in the 4: 2: 3: 1 (or the 3: 3: 3: 1) formation behind the main defenders (2: 3 or 3: 3). This last man having no special opponent to mark, has the job of coming close to the goal to the help of the left half, for example, if he is beaten by his right wing, or to the help of the centre half when the opposition centre forward has broken through. In the 4: 2: 3: 1 formation, therefore, this same specialist defender changes position and assists the rest of the defence, so that they can devote most of their attention to marking their men (see 'The Development of Team Formations' page 171).

There are many situations, however, when a back or mid-field player has moved up-field and has not returned at the correct moment, so that he is no longer able to catch the man he is supposed to be marking; then, an interchange of positions and covering becomes necessary, as described in the first example.

Fig. 109c. New Zealand demonstrated their way of zonal marking against Holland in the semi-final of the Olympic Games in Montreal

Covering in defence, by means of an interchange of positions among the defenders, used to be discussed mainly only in theory but severely neglected in practice. So as to increase sureness in defence and the self-confidence of the players, it is to be recommended, however, that covering be systematically coached with great care, aiming at a certain degree of perfection (see exercises pages 137-140).

It frequently occurs that covering is no longer possible. One defender is then left to face two attackers. In these circumstances, the defender is not necessarily recommended to try to dispossess the dribbler immediately but rather to make as if to intercept his pass in order to try and force the forward to run into the intended situation 1: 1.*

The defence gets into a similar situation when two defenders are left to face three forwards. The first method is for the two defenders to give the impression that they are going to take the dribbler and the player nearest to him; this should cause the dribbler to pass to the furthest away of his two colleagues. However, the second defender, who is not directly marking his man, is anticipating this pass. A second method is to delay the attack as long as possible by retreating in defence, so that the beaten defender can get back into position. This method, however, applies only in mid-field.

---

* see in *The Advanced Science of Hockey*' pp. 94-98.

13 The Last Line of Defence - The Theory of Coaching Goalkeepers

In hockey, the goalkeeper is one of the most important players, perhaps, even, the most important. He is the last player in the side who can prevent the ball from going into the goal and so victory or defeat can often depend on his performance. Because of his responsible function, the goalkeeper is frequently in the thick of the action and also at the centre of excited arguments. If he has had a good game, he receives applause and is showered with congratulations but, after a failure, he is severely censured by his unrelenting critics.

An excellent goalkeeper can influence a game decisively to his team's advantage, when his calmness and ability communicate themselves to the rest of the defence. His reliability gives not only his defence, but also his forwards, confidence in themselves and trust in him, qualities which can inspire the whole team to an outstanding performance and, at the same time, cripple the opposition. If, on the other hand, the last line of defence is weak and suffers from nervousness and unsureness, his influence on his team's performance is always negative, even if he does not let in a goal during the game. For instance, the forwards are then afraid to mount an attack with numerical superiority and all too easily fall back upon nervous defence.

From these few reasons, one can easily see that weaker teams with an excellent goalkeeper can produce good results against teams with excellent players but a weak goalkeeper; they can often, in fact, even beat them.

Physical and psychological considerations

So that the goalkeeper can perform his many-sided and responsible job successfully, which is in no way easier than playing anywhere else on the field, he must possess certain physical and psychological qualities and skills which set him apart from the remaining players in the side.

The most important physical consideration for a goalkeeper is speed, both of reaction and of movement, so that he is able to stop a ball hit at speeds of between 120 to 150 km/hour. But speed alone is not sufficient. It must be coupled with dexterity and flexibility. All this enables the goalkeeper to carry out defensive movements successfully, for example, a save at full stretch. Considerable muscular speed and strength is necessary to prevent the goalkeeper from being hindered in making rapid movements by his relatively heavy pads.

To develop his physical qualities to the full, the goalkeeper must also be endowed with certain psychological qualities. Courage, readiness for action, determination, strong nerves and self-confidence improve his performance, just as do great powers of concentration; of these, courage is an indispensable consideration for successful goalkeeping.

A goalkeeper who has, first of all, to overcome a moment of fear when the opposing forwards are mounting a determined attack on him or get in a hard shot at short range, will never be able to satisfy these great demands. Neither great agility, quick reactions nor skilful positional play can be put to their best advantage if courage is lacking.

Above all, the goalkeeper's nerves are put to the test, because the slightest mistake on his part can lead to a goal. To give his whole team, but especially the players immediately in front of him, confidence, the goalkeeper should endeavour to play calmly, with concentration and to act with determination, despite a certain tension before and during the game. His calmness during the course of the game should not, however, lead to a slowing down in his movements.

In his own half of the field the goalkeeper should constantly observe the situation as it develops, follow the positions and actions of both his team-mates and his opponents, but the ball must always remain the centre of his attention in order to ensure his quick reactions for a safe defence. If the goalkeeper loses sight of a shot at goal for a matter of seconds because of players running out, as frequently occurs, for instance at a penalty corner, then his reactions will certainly be slowed down for fractions of a second, thus delaying the defensive movement. As a generalisation it can be said that the goalkeeper must watch the ball carefully not only up to the point of it being struck but he must also follow it with all his concentration until he has saved it.

To build him up both physically and psychologically, the goalkeeper, in training, should be frequently played in another position, both in defence and attack. By playing out of goal, his ability to orientate himself will greatly improve, he will learn to estimate better the direction and speed of the ball and will, in the end, gain some insight into the difficulties and inhibitions of an attacker *vis-a-vis* the goalkeeper, experiences which he will put to good use later when goalkeeping. Goalkeepers who play out of goal frequently are generally mentally more alert and can anticipate many situations better than those who always remain in goal. Playing out of goal is not, however, the only training method for goalkeepers which can be used to eliminate short-comings which may occur in their understanding of the game. To do this, the detailed and lasting influence of a coach or an older experienced goalkeeper is needed in training.

By playing out of goal, and also as a result of his many years of experience in goal, the goalkeeper, with the passing of time, obtains such a good understanding of the various game situations in the circle that he is able to give directions to the players in front of him. His favourable position, from which he can observe the whole pitch, the ball and all the participants, allows him to guide the players in the immediate vicinity of his goal. The goalkeeper should always give his instructions at the correct moment, with a loud and decisive shout. Brevity is just as important as clearness and speed. There being no time for well formulated, detailed instructions he must instead use key words already previously agreed with the covering defenders.

The goalkeeper should always give his commands early enough, so that the defenders have sufficient time to carry them out.

To become a good hockey goalkeeper, a player has to train seriously, progressively and systematically for a long time. Even if physical and psychological qualities and skills can be developed and constantly improved by well planned training, the potential must, to a certain extent, be already there.

In youth teams, and sometimes even in adult teams, a player is put into goal generally because he is one of the worst field players, who perhaps does not run very well or attracts adverse attention by his clumsy movements. If, however, the full significance of the goalkeeper's contribution to his side's success or otherwise in the game is correctly recognised, then the best player in the side should be put in goal.

A goalkeeper's training is generally carried out with as little thought as his selection for the position in the first place. A goalkeeper's training should be accorded the real importance which is due to it. The sort of training which is to be seen all too frequently, even today, with the forwards hitting in at goal from the edge of the circle, is quite insufficient; this neither suits the needs of the forwards, who can happily practise shooting at goal, nor those of the goalkeeper.*

Goalkeepers should always be trained both separately (in order to ensure that sufficient attention is given to *them*), and with the rest of the team.

The following are only a few suggestions for the modern goalkeeper to follow in his training.

Exercises designed to loosen up and stretch the muscles.

Loosening and warming up the muscles serves to improve the goalkeeper's reactions and co-ordination. In the course of the match, the goalkeeper can only carry out a movement properly when he is warmed up and when, quite apart from a certain elasticity in his muscles, tendons and ligaments, there is

---

* see in '*The Advanced Science of Hockey*', chapter 'Scoring goals'

the necessary range of movement in his joints for the execution of the various movements he will be called upon to make. To enable him to make unhindered movements, the goalkeeper should incorporate special exercises in his training and warming-up which will not only improve the elasticity of his muscles, tendons and ligaments, which will have become shortened because of lack of exercise, but will help to restore the full range of movement in his joints.

1. Feet apart. Arms circling backwards and forwards gently. The same when running on the spot.
2. Running sideways with legs crossing. Feet apart. Arms outstretched at shoulder height. When running to the left the right leg is placed alternately in front of and then behind the left leg and conversely when running to the right. The steps should be kept as short as possible and be carried out as quickly as possible.
3. Leg circling. The slack knee takes control. The backswing is emphasised.
4. Feet wide apart. Trunk bending to either side. When bending to the left, the left arm slides down the left leg to touch the foot and the right arm, stretching over the head, forces the trunk further sideways to the left.
5. Feet apart. Trunk bend and touch the right heel behind the body with the left hand, without bending at the hips. Only the legs may be bent. To be carried out quickly, alternately to the left and right.
6. Feet apart. Arms held outstretched at shoulder height. Trunk bend to touch the right foot with the left hand, upright, trunk bend to touch the left foot with the right hand, upright etc. To be carried out rapidly.
7. Feet apart. Arms raised above the head. Trunk circling to the right and left. The backswing is emphasised. (Try and look at the ground behind the feet!)
8. Walking on all fours.
9. The goalkeeper sits with his legs wide apart. The trainer stands over the goalkeeper, pushing the goalkeeper's body down to his knees, and at the same time pushing his legs further apart with his feet.
10. Lunging forwards. The arms are held behind the nape of the neck. The player lunges forward alternately on the right and left leg. The forward leg forms a 90° angle between the lower leg and thigh (hurdling position).
11. Knees full bend. When crouching, one leg is swung sideways and the weight transferred onto the outstretched leg. While the weight is being transferred, the trunk must remain upright and level, and must not bob up and down. The arms are held outstretched at shoulder height. The exercise can also be carried out with a partner holding the player's hands.
12. Rapid high kicking. The trunk remains upright.
13. Swinging a leg forwards, placing it on a fence or other support, and bringing the trunk to the knees.

14. As 13, but swinging a leg sideways.
15. Hurdling position with a half turn. The goalkeeper gets into the hurdling position, raises himself, using his arms for support, so as to get back into the hurdling position after making a half turn to the side of the trailing leg. Both legs thereby alternate regularly as leading and trailing leg.
16. Trunk circling in the hurdling position with a partner sitting opposite, and hands grasped. Partner A's outstretched leading leg is placed on the bent knee of partner B's trailing leg.
17. Shoulderstand on floor with legs vertical. Alternate scissor movement of the legs, so that the toes of one foot touch the floor behind the head, whereas the other leg is taken as far as possible in the other direction (place your heel on the floor!).
18. Lying in a face-down position with the arms outstretched at shoulder level on the floor. Each leg is raised as high as possible.
19. Lying in a face-down position with the arms outstretched at shoulder level on the floor. The left (right) leg is pulled sideways across to the left (right) arm. The chest must remain touching the floor.
20. Lying in a face-up position with the arms outstretched at shoulder level on the floor. The right (left) leg is raised and pulled over the left (right) leg, so that the foot touches the left (right) hand. The shoulder must not be raised from the floor.
21. From the face-down position into the hurdling position. In the face down position the hands are level with the shoulders on the floor. The left leg is bent and pulled to the left over the outstretched right leg, while the trunk turns through 180° to the left at the same time into the sitting position.

    Then the trunk sways gently backwards and forwards over the outstretched leg. Finally, the player reverts to the face-down position and repeats the exercise with the other leg.
22. Splits position, legs well apart. The hands support the weight of the body on the floor. The trunk, which is kept as straight as possible, is moved up and down as the arms are bent and stretched. The exercise can also be carried out with a helper pressing on the shoulders.

    All these exercises can also be performed wearing pads.

*Exercises to increase flexibility and strength in the arm and trunk muscles:**

Since the nature of a goalkeeper's defensive play puts great demands on his muscular system, tensing and relaxing the muscles with great rapidity, exer-

---

* see photos in 'See and Learn Hockey' exercises for improving flexibility

cises for goalkeepers should be dynamic and designed to build up strength; they should be carried out repeatedly, as rapidly and energetically as possible, with and without pads.
1. From a position of attention the arms are flung upwards; at the end of the swing, the arms cross behind the head.
2. Press-ups. After raising the body, attempt to clap hands before the body is lowered again.
3. Press-ups. From the normal position, the player jumps alternately into a crouch and then into a straddle position.
4. Lying in a face-down position with the arms stretched out in front. Arms, trunk and legs are suddenly raised.
5. Lying in a face-down position with the arms clasped behind the neck. The trunk is raised from the floor, and abruptly twisted to the right or left, without the arms or the legs touching the floor.
6. Lying on the back, the player suddenly jack-knifes upwards with arms and legs.

Exercises to increase flexibility and strength in leg muscles. *

1. Cossack dance, with the legs kicking out sideways and forwards. Knees fully bent, one leg sideways (forwards), arms held as the player wishes. Alternate legs. The same exercise with two partners opposite each other, holding hands.
2. High kicking with one leg over the head, clapping hands underneath the outstretched leg.
3. Jump to a crouch position or jump high in the air trying to kick yourself with your heels.
4. Side lunge. Energetic, rapid sideways lunge; one arm is placed by the leading leg. The opposite leg must also be stretched.
    Practise this exercise to either side.
5. Jumping on the spot, opening and closing the legs while still in the air.
6. In a standing position; one knee is suddenly pulled up to meet the chest. Practise with left and right knees alternately.
7. Skipping on the spot. Alternately each knee is suddenly pulled up to meet the chest (and not the other way round). The trunk remains upright.
8. Rhythmic jumping with feet astride and arms outstretched.

Quickening the goalkeeper's reactions when wearing pads.

Speed of reaction is of the greatest importance for a goalkeeper. This covers the time between the goalkeeper's awareness of a situation and his eventual save. The visual perception of the situation is translated into a message which is then transmitted to the central nervous system; a response is then sent back via the motor nerves and the muscles put it into operation.

Successful goalkeeping demands the shortest possible reaction time (0.1 to 0.2 seconds). It is important to make frequent provision for reaction exercises in a goalkeeper's training programme, because results improve only slowly and because such speed of reaction as may have been acquired is soon lost by neglect. Attentiveness, self-confidence and being well rested are all factors that shorten reaction time; it is lengthened by insufficient preparation as well as tiredness, inattention, anxiety and feelings of inferiority.

1. Training with tennis balls and mini-hockey balls, first introduced by the author in 1966 and 1978, help to improve the goalkeeper's reaction time best.
2. Two goalkeepers stand facing each other 2m apart. The coach calls out the name of one goalkeeper who becomes the catcher, whereas the other tries to avoid being touched by reaching a line 10m behind him. This can also be done starting from the face downwards position, sitting, a hurdling position or lying on the back.
3. See 'Techniques when making a stop' (pages 155-161). Exercises 1-17 are particularly suitable for training reactions.

The technique and tactics of goalkeeping

Among the technical aspects which the good hockey goalkeeper must master (apart from adopting the appropriate basic position) are: basic position positional play, stopping the ball with the pads, hands or stick, as well as kicking and moving out of goal. In the following comments, apart from describing the skill concerned, the goalkeeper's tactical actions will also be considered.

The goalkeeper's position at the alert

To be prepared at any moment to make a save, the goalkeeper must adopt the appropriate basic position immediately before being called into action. For a ball hit or scooped at goal, the goalkeeper stands on his toes and should be prepared with his legs about a shoulder-width apart. This position with feet apart is necessary to preserve his balance. The legs are not straight but slightly bent, so that the goalkeeper is able to push off more rapidly with either foot. In this position of readiness, the goalkeeper must always keep his weight placed equally on both feet. In this way he avoids being caught on the wrong foot when the ball is hit at him. The upper part of the body is slightly inclined forwards at the hips, and his eyes are directed forwards at the ball. The arms are held at the side of the body and bent at the elbows in such a way that the forearms with or without the stick are pointing roughly to the base of the goal-post. Holding the arms in this way makes rapid defence with hand or stick to either side possible.

If the ball is still in the opponents' half, the goalkeeper should not remain in this position of readiness for it becomes tiring and after any length of time the muscles seize up. In order to be able to move quickly when the pressure is on, the goalkeeper needs muscles that are still supple and elastic.

Positional play

The goalkeeper must be fully aware that he is the last 'stronghold' in defence and that any mistake committed by him generally leads to a goal. If a forward makes a mistake, this does not generally have such a decisive effect on the game. But the closer the player comes to his own goal, the more dire become the consequences of any mistake committed and the greater the player's feeling of responsibility towards his whole side.

Correct positioning is vital if mistakes are to be avoided; basically, the goalkeeper should always stand on a line which bisects the angle formed by the line of the approaching ball and the line on which stand the two goal-posts (*Fig. 110*). On this bisecting line, the goalkeeper can generally save a shot at

Fig. 110. Good positional play by the New Zealand goalkeeper McHaig in a World Cup match against Malaysia.

153

goal with relatively little movement. The further he is, however, from this bisecting line, the more difficult the save becomes. Occasionally, it even becomes impossible.

But positioning himself on this bisecting line is not the only important factor in making a successful save. The goalkeeper must attempt to get as close as possible along this line to the man shooting. The closer he gets to the ball along this line, the greater will be the area that he is covering from the man shooting. If the goalkeeper is quite close to the ball, then, generally speaking, the width of his body alone is sufficient to block the way to the goal, as often demonstrated during penalty corners at the beginning of the eighties.

Exercises for coaching positional play.

1. So that the goalkeeper can learn how to position himself correctly on the line bisecting the angle, the ball is first of all dribbled by a player along the edge of the circle, and played towards the goal only after a whistle signal from the coach. The goalkeeper then has to keep on changing his relative position to the ball as the angle widens or narrows.
2. Two players standing level with the top of the circle, push the ball to each other, either while stationary or running slowly (eight to ten metres apart), prior to one of them taking a sudden shot at goal. The goalkeeper must constantly alter his position in relation to the position of the ball.
3. Short corner: the hitter-out passes the ball to one of two colleagues on the edge of the circle who attempt to score. The goalkeeper should move into a position which allows him to cover the largest area of the goal. This can also be practised with a second hitter-out from the other side of the goal.

    Variation: the player at the edge of the circle passes the ball back sometimes to the hitter-out who runs in to receive it and hits first time at goal. Here, too, the goalkeeper is required to take up his position very quickly on the line bisecting the angle as close as possible to the attacker.
4. Short corner: the hitter-out passes to the edge of the circle where several players are placed in various positions. The goalkeeper must alter his position in such a way that he can be sure of saving a ball hit at him directly or after a combination with the minimum of movement.
5. A player hits ten balls (placed at various points) at goal in rapid succession from a distance of about 12m.
6. Six to eight players with one ball are placed at various points 2m inside the circle. They each shoot at goal, at first in a predetermined order, but later in any order desired, so that the goalkeeper has to position himself

correctly on the line bisecting the angle before the shot. When the players are shooting in any desired order, it is to be recommended that they line up with their backs towards the goalkeeper. Only when the coach calls out the shooter's name, is he allowed to turn round and shoot rapidly at goal. By placing the players with their backs towards the goal, the goalkeeper then has sufficient time to enable him to face the shooter. Later on this time can be reduced.

7. Four to six players are grouped around the circumference of a circle — the circle having a radius of about 10m — and they pass the ball to each other through a goal about 5m wide made out of two posts (*Fig. 111*).

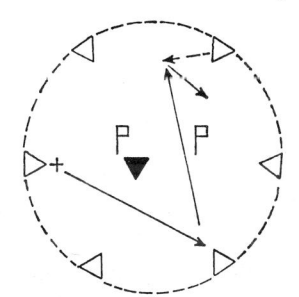

FIG. 111

The goal, which is open to attack from both sides, is guarded by a goalkeeper who must attempt to cut off as many passes as possible by means of skilful positional play. In doing so, his strides should not become too long. If he alters position with several small strides instead of one or two large ones, he can shift his weight more easily from one leg to the other, with the result that the forwards will find it very difficult to catch him on the wrong foot.

As the body-weight remains on one leg for longer when using a longer stride, the goalkeeper cannot follow swiftly enough the ever-changing situation in front of the goal.

Techniques when making a stop

Although the goalkeeper does not come into contact with the ball as often as do his team-mates in the course of the match, his training programme is, however, no less intensive.

An important aspect of the goalkeeper's many-sided training is to perfect stopping the ball with pads, hand and stick.

Stopping the ball with the pads.

The goalkeeper should achieve complete mastery of stopping the ball with his pads. Basically, he should stop the ball, keeping his legs closed, in such a way that it cannot rebound. To achieve this, the goalkeeper must bend his knees a little forwards (*Fig. 112a*).

Fig. 112a. Jose Garcia (Spain) demonstrates how to stop the ball with the pads

Fig. 112b. The opposite leg pushes the body towards the ball, so that in the moment of stopping the ball the weight of the body is positioned above the leg which stops the ball. Observe the left hand behind the left leg being prepared to help in case the ball can not be intercepted with the left pad.

A good goalkeeper will be so practised in stopping the ball that he can himself determine the extent of the rebound. For example, if an opposing forward is about 8m in front of him, he will attempt to stop the ball without any rebound, before clearing it out of the danger zone. If the goalkeeper, however, has more time and space for his save, he will allow the ball to rebound a little, so that he can clear it harder and further with a running kick.

When after stopping a shot with one leg only, the goalkeeper finds the ball close to this leg, he should then use his stick to push it away towards his teammates on the side-line. In this case it would take too long to kick clear, as the goalkeeper has first to move the outstretched leg close to the ball playing leg. Whenever the goalkeeper makes an attempt to stop the ball with one leg only, the other leg should not relax, but should push his body towards the ball, so that finally the weight of the body and the head of the goalkeeper are positioned above the vertically placed leg which stops the ball (see sequences of 'Stopping the ball' in *See and learn Hockey* and *Fig. 112b*). When stopping with the left leg, the goalkeeper should place his left hand behind the left leg; and the stick is close behind the right pad when the ball comes to the right corner of the goal. After a long stride to one side, the goalkeeper should try to place his opposite foot as close as possible beside the one which saves so that he is prepared to control the rebound in an ideal basic position.

If the goalkeeper cannot reach a shot at goal with his pads, then he has to stop the ball with his hand or stick, or even with his body.

Using his hand

The only correct method for the goalkeeper to stop the ball with his hand, without infringing the rules, is for him to catch it cleanly and release it again immediately. In this way he avoids the rebound which might occur when using the open hand. Moreover, stopping in this way avoids the possibility that the umpire will misinterpret his hand stop and award a penalty stroke, as happened to Spain in the Olympic Final, 1980, against India.

Using the stick (Fig. 123)

When stopping an individual attack with the stick on the ground or when stopping a shot towards the goal the goalkeeper should grip his light stick as high as possible in order to extend his reach to a maximum. In case the opponent changes his direction of beating him the goalkeeper should reverse his stick hold in the right hand only and put it horizontally on the ground with the hook of the blade pointing downwards.

To send the ball a greater distance out of the danger zone (by pushing, flicking or hitting), the goalkeeper must grip his stick as quickly as possible in the correct way after having stopped the ball. If the goalkeeper grips the stick in the middle with the right hand alone, he is immediately ready for action again simply by bringing his left hand onto the end of the stick. Even if he does not have time to grip with the left hand, it is still quite possible to play the ball with the right hand alone.

Drills for practising stopping shots at goal.

1. The coach stands 2m in front of the goal line, and tries to touch the line with his stick, while the goalkeeper tries to stop him from doing so. Observe the correct movement of both legs and the shift of weight towards the leg which avoids the opponent's stick from touching the line.
2. Series of pushes or shots at goal always directed to the same corner, aimed at improving and developing the goalkeeper's ball-stopping technique. Watch these points: Is his hand or stick placed behind his pad? Does he push himself as far as he can in the direction he wants to go, using the opposite leg? Is the opposite leg *fully* stretched at the moment he stops? Does he have his weight on the leg which is stopping the ball, so that the pad is vertical?
3. Flicks from 6-10m, always into the same corner at the same height, to make sure he uses the leg and hand of the same side in a correct manner.
4. The coach throws the ball into the same corner.
5. In order to quicken the goalkeeper's reactions, a tennis ball is introduced into the practice. The goalkeeper stands with his eyes closed, in the position of readiness, on the goal-line. First of all a player throws a tennis ball in the air to him from about 8-10m away. Just as the ball leaves his hands, the thrower shouts to the goalkeeper. The goalkeeper immediately opens his eyes and attempts to pick up the outline of the ball, which is already in the air, and tries to save it with his stick or hand.

    Because of its greater speed when hit at goal, and because of the reduced risk of injury for the goalkeeper (who should be practising with a helmet), a tennis ball is better suited for quickening the goalkeeper's reactions than a hockey ball, although it behaves a little bit differently in the air.
6. Hitting a tennis ball at goal from the edge of the circle. The forward shooting shouts to the goalkeeper the moment he makes contact with the ball and thereupon the goalkeeper opens his eyes. By varying the angle of the stickhead behind the ball, the shooter can easily control the

height of a shot at goal when using a tennis ball.
7. See 6 above. Shooting at the goal in all variations is practised with a mini-hockey ball (80 or 120grs).
8. Hit made with maximum force from the edge of the circle with a tennis ball (both on the ground and in the air). The goalkeeper keeps his eyes open all the time.
9. A flag is placed in front of the edge of the circle; the players run 5-6m up to the flag, beat it on one side or the other and immediately afterwards, without any further dribbling, get in a shot at goal. The second player in the line does not start to run until the man in front of him has already shot at goal.

Variation 1: To the left (right) of the shooter, a second player runs in simultaneously on the goal. His job is to put the ball rebounding from the goalkeeper's pads into the goal within three seconds (*Fig. 113*), using the forehand or reverse slap-shot with the right hand in the middle of the stick.

Variation 2: The flag can be rounded on the right by the first player and on the left by the second player or rounded according to the choice of the shooter concerned.

Variation 3: Now two flags standing 6m apart are rounded on the left, or right, or alternately. As soon as the man in front shoots at goal, the next forward starts to run.

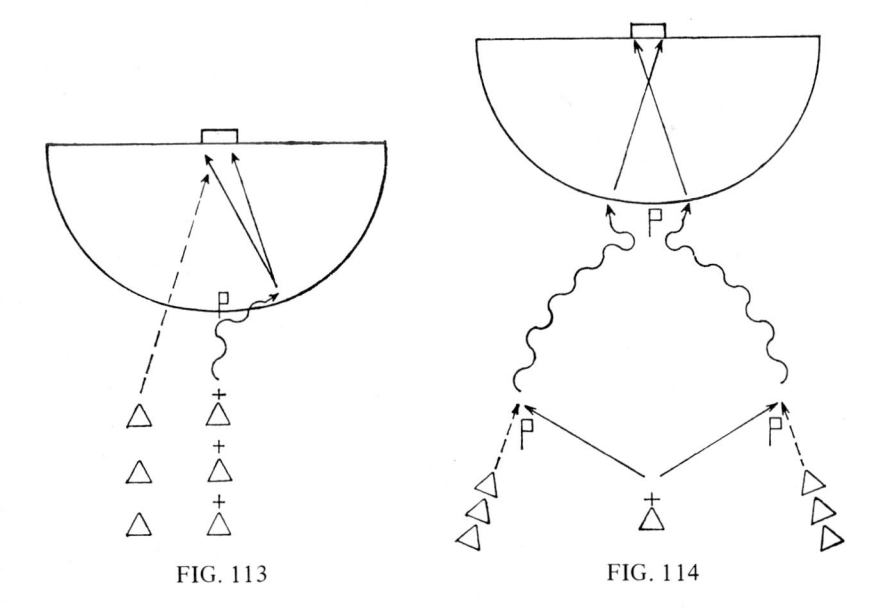

FIG. 113   FIG. 114

10. A passer pushes the ball past a flag for the inside-right to run onto. He picks the ball up on the run, rounds a second flag placed just in front of the circle on the right (left) and shoots at goal (*Fig. 114*). The passer alternately serves a player to his right and to his left.
11. A softly hit square pass is given on the edge of the circle for the inside-left to take a first time shot at goal (*Fig. 115*).
12. Two players stand on the edge of the circle. The left-back gives a moderately hit square pass (as if he had muffed the pass) to the opposition inside-left standing about 8m away (*Fig. 116*). The latter attempts to stop the ball and shoot quickly at goal, whereas the back runs after his pass and, for his part, tries to prevent the inside-left from shooting by lunging to tackle at arm's length.

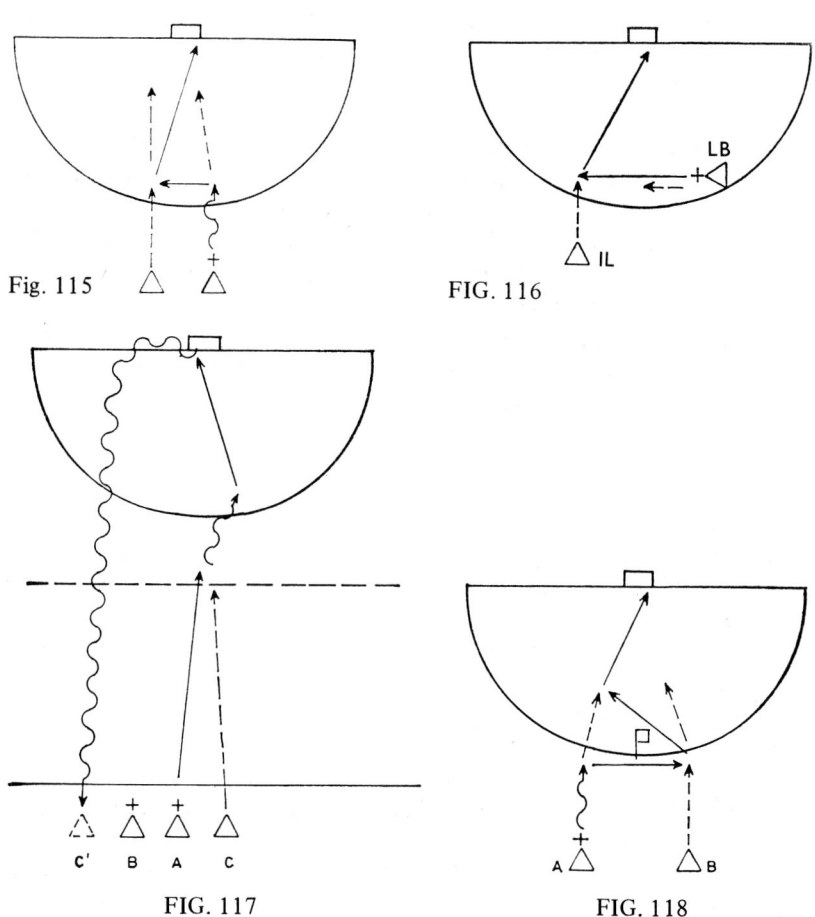

Fig. 115

FIG. 116

FIG. 117

FIG. 118

160

13. A group of three players with two balls: two players A and B stand in the middle of a field on the centre-line, each with a ball. A third player C, standing next to A, sprints off suddenly in the direction of the circle (*Fig. 117*). When A has seen what C is up to, he gives a through pass which C should run onto before reaching the circle; he then shoots at goal as he crosses the edge of the circle. Finally C collects his ball and dribbles it in a wide curve back to B. Meanwhile A has taken C's place and B has moved into A's place. This time B gives A the through pass etc.
15. 'Once Out': Four forwards play between the 22.90m line and the goal line, against two defenders and a goalkeeper. If the forwards miss the goal, or let the ball pass over any side line, two become defenders, and the backs now gain the right to attack together with two neutral attackers. The goalkeeper is neutral. The forwards also lose the right to attack if they do not score within one minute.
16. As 14, but with five forwards and three defenders.
17. Triangular passing on the edge of the circle: two players A and B run level with each other, some 4-5m apart, up to the goal. Before reaching a flag placed on the edge of the circle A squares the ball to B. Whereas A runs straight on, B plays the ball back as quickly as possible behind the flag to A with a diagonal pass (*Fig. 118*). A then shoots at goal from the inside left position.
Variation — A passive opponent comes on to take the place of the flag and has to be beaten by using the various methods of triangular passing (see 'Methodical development of the triangular pass' page 114).

Kicking

A powerful kick is eminently suitable for banishing danger from the circle and for obtaining respect from the other side. The goalkeeper must run out fearlessly and with determination, if he can be sure of reaching the ball before his opponent, and kick the ball past the opposing forward out of the danger zone. The faster he runs out to meet the ball, the greater will be the force and range of his kick. So that the goalkeeper has sufficient time to get into the correct position in relation to the ball and to swing back his kicking leg, his last stride, immediately before kicking, should always be somewhat longer. At the moment of kicking, the goalkeeper must ignore the approaching forwards and be able to direct his whole concentration and attention on the approaching ball.

Kicking, both from a stationary position and when running, demands constant practice, because it can entail considerable danger, especially on uneven pitches. The goalkeeper must not, under any circumstances, underestimate the approaching ball. Kicking a slowly moving ball demands the same care and concentration as a hard hit shot.

The goalkeeper should master kicking both with the toe and also with the instep of both feet. Even if he cannot always develop as much power with the left foot as he can with the right, he should nonetheless always be able to rely on his weaker foot in an emergency.

If an agile and speedy goalkeeper can master the technique of kicking he can then almost be regarded as a third back in the circle, and thus he makes an important contribution towards the stability and sureness of the defence.

Today extra light kickers and pads have increased considerably the power of kicking the ball.

Kicking with the toe.

Most goalkeepers prefer to kick with the toe for, in this way, correct positioning in relation to the ball is easier to assess, an unlucky bounce over the foot is rarer and it is possible to get in a harder and longer kick then with the instep.

The moment that the leg taking the player's weight lands close to the side of the ball, the kicking leg is swung backwards. The backswing takes place loosely from the hip and the leg is well bent at the knee. Simultaneously with the long swing-back of the kicking leg, the arm opposite it swings forwards, whereas the other arm moves sideways and a little behind the body in order to maintain the player's balance. The upper part of the body is well over the ball, head down and eyes directed on the ball.

The forward-swing of the kicking leg starts from the hips and it follows the direction that the ball is to go. At the beginning of the forward-swing, the upper part of the body rocks backwards a little at the hips over the leg taking the player's weight. After the kick, the foot follows the ball through as far as possible with the foot moving along the direction the ball has taken (*Fig. 119*).

Fig. 119. England goalkeeper R. Barker kicks clear in the Third World Cup

Technique of kicking with the instep.

A goalkeeper will often prefer to kick with his instep when wanting to pass to an unmarked colleague who is not too far away.

Since the ball comes into contact with the largest area of the foot, the goalkeeper can kick relatively accurately and surely with the instep.

By contrast with the toe kick, the kicking leg is now turned outwards from the hip during the swing-back, in such a way that the longitudinal axis of the foot is exactly at right angles to the direction of the kick and the sole of the boot is parallel to the ground. The leg is well bent at the knee. The downswing, which follows, starts likewise from the hips and the knee and ankle, which were kept loose at the beginning of the movement, are tensed at the moment of kicking. Just as when kicking with the toe, the goalkeeper should not check the swing-through of the leg after the kick. To achieve a degree of accuracy when passing with a kick, the foot should follow through, as far as possible, along the path of the ball.

Drills for kicking and playing in the circle:

1. Two goalkeepers, 10m apart and each defending a goal 3.66m wide, stand opposite each other and kick a hockey ball to each other. The ball may not be touched more than twice running, and if there is any infringement, a penalty kick is awarded from five metres out.
2. Chasing the ball without a stick across the width of a pitch between the 22.90m line and the centre-line, against another goalkeeper.
3. Balls hit in from the edge of the circle should be cleared after stopping or kicked first time by the goalkeeper. Five forwards in the circle try to prevent a kick into a gap.
4. The players stand in a line, each with a ball in front of the circle. The first player pushes the ball towards the goal and then runs immediately after it. The goalkeeper's job is to kick the approaching ball, with either foot, past the oncoming player in the direction of the side-line. Two small goals are erected on the side of the circle as a target through which the goalkeeper should kick the ball (*Fig. 120*).
5. The right-wing (or left-wing) dribbles to just inside the circle, and crosses the ball to the centre-forward, who is waiting for it some 5-6m in front of the goal (*Fig. 121*). From this exercise, the goalkeeper will learn to make up his mind in a flash whether to rush out of goal to pick up the centre before the centre-forward does, or whether to stay on the goal-line. To make the goalkeeper's task even more difficult, the winger should himself occasionally shoot at goal without warning. All balls

FIG. 120   FIG. 121

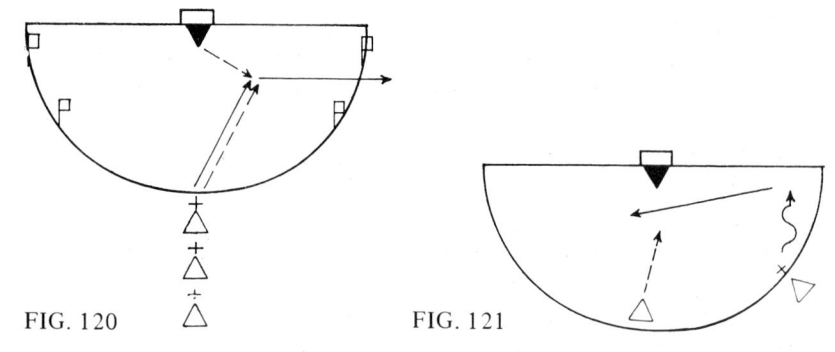

which pass closer than 3m in front of the goal should be taken by the goalkeeper.
6. Practice in running out of goal quickly to save a shot from a penalty corner, when the opponent is used to stop the ball well inside the edge of the circle.
   During this practice, the goalkeeper must take care to see that he is not running at the moment the shot is made but is standing still.
7. 8-10m in front of the goalkeeper stands a semi-passive (later an active) defender. One after another the forwards, waiting in front of the circle in a line, beat the passive defender on the right or left, and then attempt to score a goal. The goalkeeper should learn from this exercise when to stay in goal and when to leave the goal-line to narrow the angle of the shot (*Figs. 123, 124*).
8. The goalkeeper is in a square, with sides which are 8m long. Forwards who have lined up one behind the other, 6m in front of the square, attempt to round the goalkeeper within the square.
   If, during the forwards' attempts to beat the goalkeeper, the ball goes off over either side-line to right or left, or if the goalkeeper manages to defend the second or rear line, then he receives a point. If the forwards succeed in dribbling the ball over the rear goal-line, then they receive a point. Whoever has the greater number of points after 20 (30) quickly executed attacks, is the winner.
9. The coach stands in the goal and plays the ball to the goalkeeper, who tries to kick with either foot the ball from the edge of the circle back into the goal.

The 'save-clear'

Due to the introduction of new equipment in the late 70s (especially high density foam kickers) the method of stopping the ball dead and then clearing it with the use of the stick or either foot to an unmarked team-mate or an unoccupied area was more and more replaced through the 'save-clear'. Especially in situations where the opponent, once the initial shot was taken, is very close to the goalkeeper in order to take the offensive rebound, this technique has obviously a big advantage as only one movement (save) is required instead of two.

Instead of waiting and then cushioning the ball with the body weight over the non-saving foot (which results in the goalkeeper falling backwards and which furthermore prevents him from reaching out sufficiently with his ball saving foot so that he is unable to reach the goalpost), the goalkeeper attempts to approach the ball ½m in front of his playing foot with the body weight transferred forward to that side until his knee and head are above the ball. The transfer of body weight over the saving foot enables balance to be maintained, the ball to be kept down and power to be produced through the ball in the direction of the clearance. A well timed 'save-clear' uses the power of the initial shot (together with the characteristics of the specific equipment) to save and distribute the ball away from the danger zone in one complete movement.

The 'save-clear', a technique first developed in England by David Vinson, should be applied also for raised shots towards the left or right with the exception that now the full face of the pad is offered pointing towards the oncoming ball.

The goalkeeper's role in the circle

The opportunity frequently arises for the goalkeeper to take an active part in the game outside the goalmouth (but still within the circle). If the ball is missed by his own defence, and if, in the view of the goalkeeper, no other defender can reach the ball first, he must take it himself. He must run out as quickly as possible towards the ball and kick it back upfield. In doing this, the goalkeeper should not kick it straight upfield, but, whenever possible, should send it off in the direction of the sidelines so as to avoid giving it to an opponent, and thereby, perhaps, present him with a chance to score.

The goalkeeper finds himself in a much more difficult situation when an opposing forward is bearing down alone at goal, with the ball fully controlled (*Fig. 122*). In this case, the goalkeeper has to act really fast. If there is the slightest chance of another defender intervening and preventing the shot at goal, then the goalkeeper should stay in the goal. If, however, in his judgement this is impossible, then, in accordance with the principle of narrowing the angle, he must quickly get down in front of the forward so that his completely outstretched body forms a right angle with the forward's pene-

Fig. 122. To beat a goalkeeper who is running out, it is usually more successful to pass the goalkeeper on his reverse side rather than on his right. A moment after this picture was taken Willem Klomp scored for the Netherlands against Belgium in an inter-nations military match, because the goalkeeper did not act as the ones in Figs. 51d, 123 and 124

tration (*Fig. 124*). If the goalkeeper, whose dexterity and speed are reduced by his pads, risks going out as far as the edge of the circle, the forward's chances of beating him increase considerably, because of the larger area which he then has at his disposal.

The most frequent mistakes committed by the goalkeeper are as follows:
1. They stick too much to the goal-line and do not take part in the general play.
2. They run out unnecessarily or too early, as, for instance, when the situation could be dealt with by another defender.
3. Lack of understanding between the goalkeeper and his colleagues. If the goalkeeper has decided to run out to meet the ball, then no other defender should get in his way. In this situation he should let his colleagues know of his intentions by giving a short, precise and, above all, loud shout.
4. Forwards who have perfect close control of the ball are tackled with one foot: instead, they should immediately block the forward's path, laying down very close to the forward parallel to the goal line (i.e. back to it), with the stick held higher than normal to provide an extended reach (see *Fig. 123*).
5. They slide onto the ground to save, when the forward in possession does not have the ball close to the curve of his stick.
6. They kick or hit the ball straight to an attacker, because their kick or clearing hit does not go into unoccupied space.

Fig. 123. Instead of blocking the Indian forward's path, by laying down parallel to the goal line, Jose Garcia, in the 1980 Olympic Final, uses unsuccessfully the sliding tackle, but fortunately saves the situation by making use of his stick.

Fig. 124. Jose Agut (Spain) rushing out of goal to avoid the Pakistan forward's use of the reverse stick flick whilst the sweeper de Frutos blocks a possible counter move towards the reverse stick side of the goalkeeper.

7. They dive, head first, out of goal.
8. In defending their goal, they all too often fall to the ground and frequently backwards because they forget to transfer the weight of the body towards the ball playing leg or position themselves flatfooted.
9. They use a too heavy stick which they often forget to grip high enough.
10. They are not using a helmet and chest protector.

Defending a penalty stroke

When a penalty stroke has been awarded, the goalkeeper's positional play is restricted in certain respects by the rules. The rule which states that the goalkeeper must stand with both legs on the goal-line until the stroke is taken prevents him from leaving his line in order to narrow the angle of the shot.

What can the goalkeeper do to save a penalty stroke? Many goalkeepers immediately throw themselves towards one corner without any consideration for the direction of the ball, so as to make a save easier if the ball does in fact go in that direction. Although countless penalty strokes can be saved in this way, this method is not to be recommended without question. Rather, the goalkeeper should consider an alternative.

If the ball is flicked hard and very close to the goal post, the prospects of the goalkeeper making a successful save are very poor. If, however, the opponent does not flick the ball so hard or if he flicks it nearer the middle of the goal, then the goalkeeper's chances improve. In defending a penalty stroke, the goalkeeper should start, therefore, from the assumption that he will hardly ever be able to save a ball flicked close to either of the goalposts, whereas he will perhaps succeed in saving a badly flicked ball. From that derives the practical conclusion that the goalkeeper must do everything to induce the person taking the penalty stroke into making a mistake (i.e. flicking inaccurately).

How then can the goalkeeper induce his opponent into making a mistake? Firstly, he should radiate confidence in front of the player taking the penalty stroke. Secondly, he can stand in the basic position and spread his arms out a little to either side and move them up and down. By doing this, the goal will appear smaller to the opponent, who will perhaps be a little put off and feel less sure of himself than previously. Finally, just before the penalty stroke is carried out, the goalkeeper can pass the stick from the left to the right hand. Under certain circumstance, the penalty stroke taker will be disturbed in his concentration just before taking the penalty by this action; conditions have suddenly changed and, instead of putting the ball into his favourite spot in the goal, say, the top right hand corner, the player will change his mind, with adverse affect on his effectiveness.

The player taking the penalty stroke can also make a deceptive movement first. If the goalkeeper, however, keeps his attention centred on the ball and the direction it takes, he will not be taken in by any deception on the part of the penalty stroke taker (his stance or position of his stick).

When defending a penalty stroke the goalkeeper should always stay on his feet and not try to act similar to a handball goalkeeper diving into one corner for which no time is available in hockey (*Fig. 125*).

The goalkeeper's dress

Is the colour of the goalkeeper's shirt of no real consequence? Should the goalkeeper put on a sweater with striking colours, and if so, why? Should the goalkeeper paint his pads white?

These questions are in no way superfluous, for the colour of the goalkeeper's dress has a real psychological as well as tactical importance. A forward, bearing down on his opponent's goal, will be concentrating his attention mainly on the ball while shooting. An experienced player, trained to use his peripheral vision, will be able to notice, quite apart from the ball, the movements of the goalkeeper, or, at least, he will be aware of where he is standing. If the player does succeed, in the course of shooting, in also register-

Fig. 125. A penalty stroke seen from the Australian goalkeeper's point of view, during the Fourth World Cup match against Poland

Fig. 126. The penalty stroke seen from the attacker's point of view, although the goalkeeper holds the stick in his left hand the wrong way the attacker tries to score to his right.

ing the goalkeeper's positional movements, he will obviously try to take the goalkeeper's position into account when aiming, so as to be able to score.

Goalkeepers should take this fact into account. They can do this, firstly, by not making any unnecessary movements, especially to either side, because moving figures are noticed sooner and more clearly by peripheral vision than are still figures. Secondly, the goalkeeper can camouflage his positional play and movements to a certain extent, if he chooses the colour of his clothing correctly.

The majority of hockey goalkeepers dress in colours which contrast sharply with the background. They justify this by claiming that striking colours serve as an aiming point and attract the ball straight to the goalkeeper. This view can only be maintained when dealing with inexperienced attackers. For a player who has been coached well, both technically and tactically, the goalkeeper, who stands out well from the background, represents a good aiming point for accurate shooting.

Experience teaches, therefore, that the goalkeeper should choose the colour of his pads and of his shirt from the tactical point of view, in such a way that the colour blends in with the background and surroundings. By means of this camouflage, the attacker will experience greater difficulty in using his peripheral vision to make out the position of the goalkeeper at all accurately or quickly. He cannot find an aiming point for accurate shooting, so that the goalkeeper's chances of making a successful save are increased.

14 The Development of Team Formations

When Harrow brought out the first hockey rules in 1852 (among others, was the one that not more than thirty players could take part on each side), there was naturally, as yet, no real system in the play. The individual players had no specific positions and no special function. Today we would consider that they merely hit the ball carelessly upfield.

The first traces of a team formation

Even before the turn of the century, the first traces of a team formation are recognisable. The teams were divided into two divisions, each according to the sort of task it had to perform, into a defensive and an attacking division, in which the latter was always numerically superior (nine to two, eight to three or seven to four). Instead of the ball being hit haphazardly in the direction of the other circle, some attempt was now made, as a consequence of this distribution of tasks, at combining the team's efforts. When, still before the first World War, an attempt was begun, for tactical reasons, to put an end to the numerical superiority of the forward line, the development of the modern formation began.

The 'pyramid'

The pyramid was the first modern team formation. It was used with only minor changes until about 1960 and is still to be seen in a few teams.

This sytem was founded on a numerical balance between defenders and attackers.

In front of the goal-keeper, two backs and three halves try to protect their goal against an attack composed of five forwards (*Fig. 127*). In the first line of defence were two 'home-based' backs, who generally wait at the edge of the circle for the attack to come to them. They often intervene only when the second line of defence, the half-back line, had been beaten. In contrast to the wing halves, however, the centre half's role was fairly free. When the centre half was not occupied in defence, he frequently reinforced the attack, acting as a sixth forward. The five forwards all attacked in line abreast.

Very soon disadvantages began to appear with this line-up. On the one hand, it allowed a gap to appear between the lines of attack and defence, thus favouring the opponents in attack; on the other hand, however, it made the

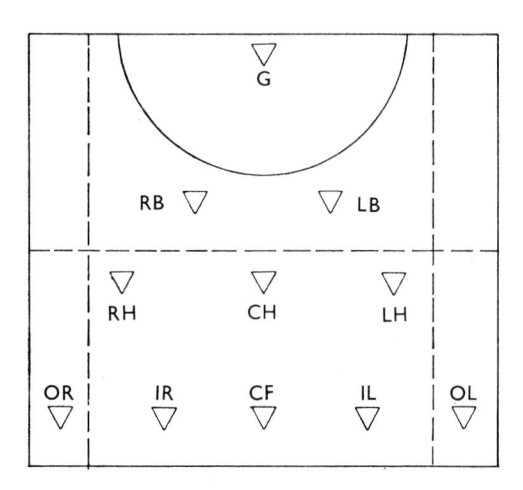

FIG. 127

work of the opposing defence somewhat easier. If the ball was lost during an attack, then all five forwards were eliminated from the game at a stroke. These disadvantages were soon removed by pulling back two of the five forwards, the two insides, with the result that there was more depth in the attack. In this way, the development of a team formation was taken a step further. Passing, as a result of this greater depth in attack, became richer in variety and consequently, defending became more difficult.

The concept from 1962 onwards

From about 1960 a few teams began to feel discontented with the division of the players' responsibilities which had been generally accepted until then, especially because of the problems occurred in defence through the superiority of the number of attackers. In the past, the inside forwards had been given too much room for their attacks, because the backs used to hang so well back. Apart from the defenders' own inside forwards, only the centre half could engage the inside trio at an early stage and he, generally, ran from one inside forward to the other, with the result that he was frequently beaten.

His intervention, however, was not entirely wasted for it made defence somewhat easier for his backs who had a good rest.

The covering of the gaps, too, proved unsatisfactory in certain parts of the field against opposing forwards in the course of an actual match. A defence, drawn up skilfully in echelon, marking the forwards as early as possible, should be able to give relief in this case. A few timid attempts to allow the wing halves to mark the inside forwards and to entrust the opposing wingers to the backs did not produce the desired results. On the contrary, long passes

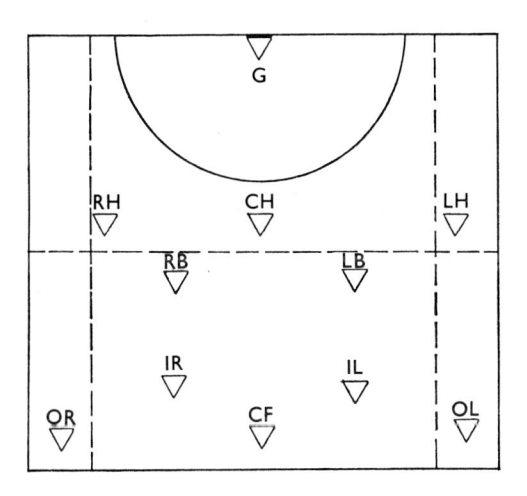

FIG. 128

became very effective and slow coverers were frequently over-run by the faster forwards.

In 1961-62 there emerged, at last, a new, simple and effective concept. In this new system, which the German national side adopted so successfully in Ahmedabad 1961, Lyon 1963 and also, in 1966, in Hamburg, the rear line of defence was formed by the wing halves and the centre half, (*Fig. 128*). The right half marks the left wing, the centre half the opposing centre forward and the left half the right wing. In the front line of defence are the two 'backs', in front of the 'halves' and behind the forwards (*Fig. 128*). Their primary task is to reduce the great area which both opposing inside forwards have had, until now, at their disposal, by being able to meet their man at an early stage. The forward line now consists of two lines. The inside forwards, who hang back, have largely the job of building up an attack. Apart from their primary task of attack, they must also join in the defence against their opponents' attack. The three forwards lying further upfield, the two wings and the centre-forward, are used almost exclusively in attack.

This system is simple: the players' tasks are clear and relatively easy to carry out. Its great advantage, as opposed to the pyramid system, is its flexibility, which leads to greater safety, especially in defence. The numerical balance, in comparison with the opposing attack is maintained, with the difference only that, in this system, the disposition of the players on the pitch has been altered.

In further explanation of the general defensive tactics of the system, it must be pointed out that the centre-half generally operates behind his wing halves and backs, because he is forced to greater caution, as a consequence of his central position. The reason being that, an opponent who breaks through the middle represents the greater danger to the goal. By positional play, the centre half prevents the opposing centre forward from reaching the ball passed into the gap sooner than himself. In addition, the withdrawn position of the centre-half lends itself especially well, if the opposing forwards are faster, to allowing the centre half to help out his wing halves and backs when they are beaten. His withdrawn position does not mean, however, that the opposing centre forward is always available for a pass. If the pass to the centre forward is a long distance one, then the centre half generally has time, because of the length of the pass, to move up to mark him or, at least, to take him just as he is trying to bring the ball under control.

If the centre half has got sufficiently used to his opponent and knows that he is faster than him, he can alter his position somewhat. In this case, he should get closer to the centre forward, so as to be able to nip an attack in the bud at the earliest possible moment.

If the ball is out on the right wing, instead of in the middle of the field, the defence alters its collective position. Now the defenders line up diagonally (*Fig. 129*).

The left half engages the opposing right wing, who is dribbling with the ball. To support their half, the left back, as well as the centre half, moves backwards a little and to the left, while the right back comes back furthest of all and now stands a good eight metres away from his opponent, the inside left. If the ball is now crossed to the left wing, then the defence takes up new positions in accordance with the changed circumstances.

This diagonal line-up is best suited, from the defensive point of view, for dealing with a breakthrough, since the opponent bearing down at goal must

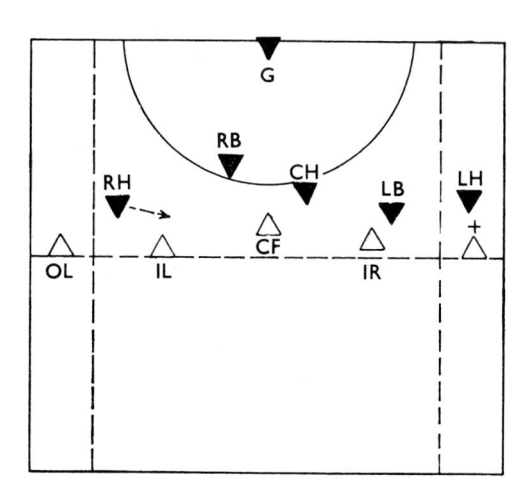

FIG. 129

get through three lines of defenders, thus providing defence in great depth, before he is able to get in a shot at goal.

If, for example, the right wing manages to beat the left half, then the left back or also the centre half (in case the left back is unable to take up his position on the diagonal line in time) can easily get in the way of the right wing as he breaks through. The backing up is completed by the right back who comes well back (forming almost the last line in defence) and who moves in towards the middle a little. He can, therefore, leave his position without great risk, because the square pass from the right wing to the inside left takes so long that the right back is given time to regain his position and take on his inside left again. Moreover, the right half can also take on the inside left, as he is trying to bring the long square pass under control.

The rather loose covering described above gives way to much tighter covering, the nearer the opponents are to the circle. Despite this, the centre half should always maintain his central position; theoretically, he is the last player outside goal to meet any forward breaking through.

As this system continued to develop, some important disadvantages, both in attack and also in defence, began to appear, however. These disadvantages were made especially clear on fast, hard pitches or in matches against teams who knew how to reduce time consuming dribbling to a minimum and to play the ball quickly from one man to another. As these disadvantages (especially when the point of attack was suddenly changed with a square pass from one front man to another) became more and more obvious, it was natural that an attempt should be made to put an end to them.

The 4: 2: 3: 1 formation (introduced in 1965 by the author to match the world's top sides, India and Pakistan) with a rather different division of duties for the individual players, especially for the centre half and the centre forward, can be regarded as the last big change in the development of team formations, because the 3: 3: 3: 1 and 2: 4: 3: 1 systems are developments from it.

The 4: 2: 3: 1 system

The central figure in the old system was the centre half. His job was not only to mark the opposing centre forward but also to control the middle section of the pitch in front of goal. The centre half, however, was over-burdened by this double task. He could only fulfil it when his man remained constantly in position running down the middle of the field.

If, however, the centre forward moved off to one side or the other, the centre half was forced to decide which of his two tasks was the more important: to mark his man tightly or to cover the open space. If he followed his man, he then left this area in front of goal free, into which other opponents might suddenly run. If, however, he covered this central area in front of goal, he had to leave the centre forward unmarked, who could then go where he liked. That, in addition to the centre half having to mark the opposing centre forward, he also had attacking functions to fulfil – his role was the most attacking among the defenders' in the pyramid system – was tactically incomprehensible.

This weakness in the old system could be corrected by dividing the centre half's duties among two players. This move was the key to the new formation.

To change over to the new system, the centre forward must be pulled back and take on the task of marking the opposing centre forward, whereas the centre half, now freed from this duty, operates behind the rest of the defence and blocks the most direct path to goal (*Fig. 130*). By these means, both the backs can be sent further upfield in front of the halves, so as to take on the opposing inside-forwards at the earliest possible moment, and to join the attack with almost no risk for the defence.

A diagonal line-up, or a formation where players interchange positions with all its attendant disadvantages, is no longer necessary. Both backs are now to remain constantly in the immediate proximity of the man they are marking, playing now more aggressive and attacking hockey.

Often one of the two backs leaves his forward entrusted to his care when his own side gains possession of the ball in order to move into the attack (*Fig. 131*).

There are four attacking forwards and their only defensive duties are to mark any opposing half or full back moving up into the attack from out of the opposing defence.

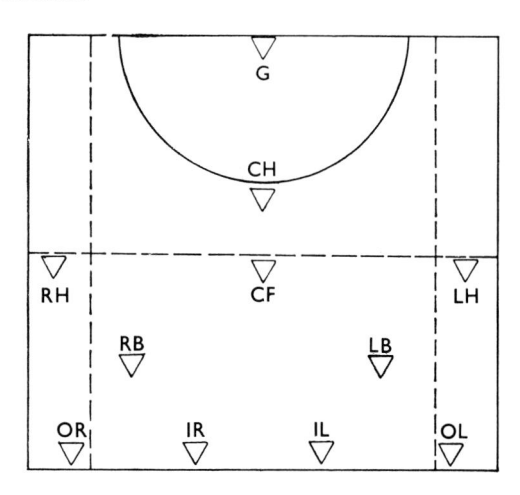

FIG. 130

FIG. 131

FIG. 132

The wing halves' function is as defensive as offensive, in that their main task is to cut out the opposing wings. Since the centre forward is well back, keeping an eye on the opposing centre-forward, the whole of the opposing attack is marked man for man at the earliest possible moment. It has no space free for manoeuvre.

The distinctive feature of this system is the position of the centre half (sweeper) who remains behind the two wing halves and the centre forward (even though he is well back), as well as behind the two backs; above all, he has no specific man to mark. He positions himself generally on the 22.9m line, moving to left and right across the whole width of the pitch. His task is to pick up the through passes, which are encouraged by his side's close marking, and to assist his own backs and halves in repairing any breakdown in defence (*Fig. 132*).

For a better understanding, we must go into the defensive play of this system rather more closely. Both backs must constantly interfere with the build-up work of the opposing inside forwards as soon as the opposition gains possession. To mark them closely without covering the space does not produce any risk, because, in the case of a break-through, there is always the centre-half or the 'sweeper' to take on the opponent. When their own forwards have the ball, the backs should position themselves in front of their opponents, so as to take part in the attack. A back pass to the backs, or the so called mid-field players or link men, from one of their own forwards must always be made possible. When the ball is lost, the link men must then immediately search out their opposite numbers and place themselves directly behind them.

For this reason, at least one of the two link men should move upfield into the forward line only up to a position that would allow him at any time to revert to marking the opposing inside forward, if his own side's attack is halted. If he is unable to do this, then the sweeper, who is hanging well back, in co-operation with his other team-mates takes on his opponent. If the link man has been beaten in midfield, he should tackle back again. If the sweeper, however, has to intervene in the place of the beaten link man, then the link man should take over, as quickly as possible, both the position and the duties of the sweeper. The primary function of link men remains defence. They should only take part in the attack when they do not endanger their own side's defence by so doing. If one were to try and express the apportionment of the link man's work load between attack and defence in terms of figures, one would say that sixty per cent is devoted to defence and forty per cent to attack. Naturally these figures are only a rough approximation. The proportion does not depend only on the running ability of the link man concerned, but also on his individual inclinations and his own tactical outlook. There are link men who are naturally inclined towards attack — normally they have been inside forwards at some time — and also link men who prefer to assist more in defence. Generally speaking, the two link men have no equal division of duties between attack and defence. Whereas the right link man will concern himself more with attack, the left link man will be more concerned with eliminating the opposing inside-right, on whom, so often, the opposition attack will be founded.

The advantages of the system, as opposed to earlier systems, are as follows:
1. The constant movement of the backs up and down the field — a method which was never entirely satisfactory because it caused great anxiety in defence against fast forward lines who could combine successfully — has now become superfluous. The backs (link men), as well as the man marking the opposing centre-forward (centre-half), can now leave to the sweeper, who hangs well back, as a sort of reserve back, their task of

covering, which earlier had made necessary the temporary abandonment of their opposite number.
2. A cover which has depth and is relatively flexible leaves the opposing forwards little room and time for developing their attack. Three players in defence, one after another, must all fail if a goal is to be scored against them from open play: i.e. the defender responsible for looking after the forward as he breaks through, the reserve back and the goalkeeper.
3. As the sweeper plays behind the defensive line of 5 players, the use of the off-side trap is made much easier than before.
4. By rapid changes of position, the side endeavours always to have one more player in attack or defence than the opposition. It is no longer a matter of playing with only four forwards, but frequently with five or even six. In contrast to earlier formations, the four forwards are putting all their effort into attack the whole time. For the development of their attacks, there is more room available across the width of the pitch than was the case earlier.
5. A change in the line-up of the forwards takes place automatically when one or two link men or halves move up into the attack. Defence is thus made more difficult for the opposition.
6. The workload is now almost evenly distributed among all the ten players playing out of goal.
7. Because of the five line formation, combined play is made easier. The short pass is now preferred to long passes, which are easier for the opponents to pick up. This does not mean, however, that the long pass, which can so unexpectedly switch the point of attack, can be done away with. Rather, because of the greater number of lines in the team formation, the ball is more frequently played backwards.

A very important condition for success with this different disposition of the forces on the pitch is that the team should possess three excellent 'keymen', who can fulfil the general and specific tasks of the sweeper and of the two link men.*

No system endures

Finally it must be said that no system in hockey can be expected to endure. The 4: 2: 3: 1 system was replaced in 1974 by the 3: 3: 3: 1 system,* with rapid surprise attack as its more important tactical aspect.

---

* see in *'The Advanced Science of Hockey'* chapter 'Team tactics for the 3: 3: 3: 1 formation'

Four years later, the Spanish National Team successfully adopted the 2: 4: 3: 1 system in the 3rd World Cup, 1978 using the fourth link man as the free man in mid-field. The so called 'fireman system' was perfected until 1984 with the 'fireman' playing basically further up in line with the two front runners leading, therefore, again to the 3: 3: 3: 1 system with a different task for the field players compared with the traditional 3: 3: 3: 1;

But, after 1986, hockey players will reflect and experiment further, especially when the F.I.H. one day agrees to change three basic rules of the game like —
1. abolition of the circle (goals can be scored only from inside the 22.90m zone) which would also change positively the set up of the penalty corner
2. abolition of the off-side rule
3. allowance to change players as practised in indoor hockey

With or without the necessary rule changes the players will no longer be divided up in an orderly manner as forwards, halves, link men and sweepers. Then forwards will help out in their own circle and defenders will be scoring goals. In fact, we have already moved very close to this system for the players' tasks in their various positions resemble each other more and more. Already most of the top players go on the attack, as soon as their side gains possession of the ball, and all the players fall back on defence, as soon as their side loses the ball. The only real use for a line-up then will be to tell anyone interested who is actually playing and not in which position he is playing. The player's position on the field will depend more on each situation as it arises, quite independent of the number on their shirt and of the team line-up as it will appear in the programme.

15 What is 'Modern' Hockey?

European and especially Australian hockey has caught up with Asian hockey. If their speed of the game's development continues as it has done in the last decade, and Asian hockey continues to stagnate and resist the new European and Australian impulses, then Europe and Oceania could overtake Asia in the very near future.

Yet if the Indians and Pakistanis will learn from their former students — especially in regard to new tactical aspects — then another Olympic final between India and Pakistan is inevitable. The gold medal favourite for the Olympic Games and World Cup titles will be the European, Asian or Oceanic team which has learned to play really modern hockey.

What does 'modern' hockey tactically mean? As I see it, the main characteristics are:
1. Offensive interpretation and planning of the game of hockey.
2. Mutual understanding between the players through 'cues' in order to ensure for instance that the passer knows exactly when, how and where to pass the ball.
3. Fast switches from defence to attack and vice-versa.
4. Short duration attacks with a small number of passes. Because counter attacks are more effective, they should have preference to positional attacks.
5. Making use of close marking within one's own half.
6. Not permitting the opponents too much space and time to develop their game.
7. Creation of space through fast transfers of pressure in the width and depth of the field, well timed interchanging of positions between two and three players in a precise moment and diagonal runs in the opposing defence with support from the second attacking line.
8. Continuous support of the player who is in possession of the ball.
9. Organised and systematic taking of a rebound after a shot at the opponent's goal and following up the solo attacker.
10. Dictating the rhythm of the game.

The national team which wants to attain the world's leading position, besides having high technical maturity, strong qualities of will in individual players, who know to attack and defend, and very good physical fitness in speed, endurance, stamina and dexterity must learn the tactic of fast counter-attacks.* To achieve this, a team leaves the midfield to the less skilful opponents. This means that one's defence does not begin harassing or tackling at the moment of losing the ball in the opponent's half but in one's half only. All players, with the exception of one or two forwards, must retreat to their own half immediately they have completed an attack.

Because of tight and immediate marking the opponents will be forced, especially in the space between the 22.90m and the centre-line, to make mistakes from which the team can immediately mount fast counter-attacks.

The counter-attacks must be swift since the opponent's forwards have come all the way into your half of the field. Their effectiveness depends on the speed of their construction. Every one of the defenders who obtains possession of the ball, must try to start a new attack as fast as possible. His first pass must be made without any time-consuming dribbling. Only in a desperate emergency, such as when a defender is still being harassed, is a short dribble permitted before distributing the ball.

If possible, a long pass should be played to one of the forwards in the centre line in order to cross the whole midfield as fast as possible. The forwards who are lying up, have not been committed to defensive action and so should be fresh and able to continue the fast attack.

A second very important function for the defensive players is to sprint out of their own half to support their attack in order to achieve an equality or even superiority of players in attack.

Speed is vital

The midfield must be crossed with great speed. The outplayed opposing forwards and defenders must not have time to head back and reform. If an attack that goes the length of the field, is not concluded in eight seconds, then usually a good opposing team is able to organise its defence quickly enough to block that attack.

A point to bear in mind is that if your opponents attack with few players, then one's defending players should not hit long passes to their forwards. It is better to keep the ball in a superior defence with short passes without trying to cover space.

When short passes within one's own half induce the opponents to come out of their defensive shell, then, without warning, an attack should be started

---

* see in 'The Advanced Science of Hockey', chapter 'Theory and Practice of Counter Attacks'

Fig. 133. Saminllah (Pakistan) concludes a counter attack against England in the Champions Trophy.

with a long, exact pass covering the midfield. Simple passes, especially through balls or long fast dribbling, will then help to finish such fast attacks successfully, as the attackers will have more space for their actions and more chance of success than they would have against a massive and well-organised defence.

The more a team presses another team into its own half, the easier it is for the defending eleven to intercept the action of the attacking forwards. Besides the defending team can themselves surprise with fast breaks.

The fast attack should become a decisive element in every game. It must not be introduced casually but systematically.*

Speed, hard and exact passes, running without the ball, to assist the player in possession and secure fast dribbling, are the requisites necessary to achieve the aim of getting into the opponents' circle with the least number of passes. Having already the physical fitness and the technical skills, the team that hopes to win the highest awards must make use of fast breaks. It can do this only by training its talented players methodically with this tactic.

Perfection in this movement must be the aim of all ambitious teams.

16 The Player's Style of Running

The way the hockey player runs differs in some respects — especially when he approaches the ball — from the way the athlete runs. Since the hockey player, for his part, must always be ready to be able to change direction, the length of his stride cannot be as great as that of the sprinter or the long distance runner. The hockey player generally has to place his foot straight down beneath him when running, whereas the athlete strives to step in front of the vertical axis of his body. To make it easier to halt or turn quickly, the hockey player should attempt, in addition, to keep his centre of gravity fairly close to the ground. An exception to this occurs, however, when he has to sprint over quite a long distance, say thirty to fifty metres, when he does not then need to worry so much about changes in direction or a sudden stop. When he is sprinting towards the ball in these circumstances, the player will run with long strides, just as an athlete does, to cover the ground.

The hockey player's style of running is, of course, somewhat impaired by his having to carry a stick. Nonetheless, so as to achieve a co-ordinated, harmonious and economical style of running, the player who has to run at speed for more than, say, ten metres to the ball, should hold the stick in the middle, with the right hand alone, for the following reasons:

1. Since the right hand grips the middle of the stick in stopping, pushing and flicking, as well as in tackling, the player is immediately ready for action merely by bringing the left hand quickly onto the end of the stick.
2. The weight of the stick is most easily borne when the stick is gripped in the middle; gripping the stick at the end not only entails a bad distribution of weight but also impairs the free swinging of the arm when running. Only directly before making a reverse-stick tackle must the defender make the best of these disadvantages, as he then grips the stick at the end with his left hand alone in the last few metres before making the tackle.
3. Holding the stick with the left hand in the middle when running is uneconomical, because the player then has not only to alter the grip with his left hand in order to play the ball, but also has to bring the right hand onto the stick to grip it in the middle, which makes a second and extra movement.

In order to achieve as high a running speed as possible, both arms, as well as the hockey stick which is held in the right hand, should swing at the player's sides, along the direction that the player is running and not across

Fig. 134. Running with one hand on the stick is both economical and harmonious. Contrasting styles by Marie Birtwistle of England (white shirt) and Steffi Drescher of Germany.

his chest (*Fig. 134*). Only when the player nears the ball does the right hand guide the stick across the body, in such a way that the end of the stick is moved towards the left hand.

Only from players carrying the stick in one hand can we expect a certain relaxation in their running, a decrease of tension and an evenness in their movement as well as a very high speed of running. None of these things is possible, however, with a player who carries his stick in both hands while running (*Fig. 134*). He runs in an awkward, ungainly way using too great a degree of power, which is only too obvious; or, as a lorry driver would say, he is 'driving with the hand-brake on'. Many muscles, particularly in the arms and shoulders, which are really not involved and should remain relaxed, are tensed when the stick is carried in both hands. When a player runs with both hands holding the stick, the arms are then swung across the chest which produces considerable movement of the shoulders. This use of the shoulders leads to a twisting of the spine, which then interferes with the player's co-ordination as he runs and consequently reduces his speed.

The hockey player should learn from the best sprinters in the world today who run with their shoulders relaxed and almost motionless. This is possible, however, only when the stick is held in the right hand alone while running.

17 Developing Flexibility and Dexterity

A player's flexibility depends on the extent his limbs can swing from the joints and on his motor apparatus. The hockey player should increase it by means of gymnastic (stretching) exercises. Since the use of these exercises alone will not strengthen the muscles or ligaments and will adversely affect a player's bearing, the stretching of certain groups of muscles should be done by exercises which also strengthen them (e.g. using a medicine ball or with a partner).

By dexterity we mean the good co-ordination of the entire motor system of the body (Meinel). In order to increase the player's dexterity, his experience of possible movements must be so widened that he can immediately adapt himself, quickly and successfully, to the ever changing situations which occur during a match. Flexibility and dexterity are closely related but, for purely instructional reasons, they are dealt with separately here. A characteristic of hockey is the multiplicity of skills involving movement; running forwards, sideways and backwards with or without the ball, coming to a sudden halt, dodging and body swerves; in addition, there are the movements peculiar to hockey such as the push, the hit, the stop, the flick and the dribble to mention but a few. Modern hockey demands that the player not only masters all these movements and understands exactly when to use them but also that he can perform them quickly and as accurately as possible.

Agile and sprightly players who are capable of following each situation as it arises by skilful and lightning quick movements have a great advantage over those players who, for instance, are not agile enough to shake off the man, who is marking them out of the game, or to do the same to an opposing forward. For a forward to be able to escape from the man marking him or for a defender to be able to mark his opposite number out of the game, the player, apart from being a top class runner, needs flexibility and dexterity, qualities which are displayed in sudden stops, unexpected changes in direction, body swerves, surprise variations in speed etc.

Asians and Africans are vastly superior to us in carrying out these movements, thanks to their flexible and relaxed muscular system, which is capable, however, of sudden contraction, and to their joints which allow a great range of action. The dexterity and flexibility of the Asians can only be matched if players manage to acquire, by means of training, all the most important skills and then make appropriate use of them firstly in practice games and then, later, in a match.

To start with, the hockey player must get used to a style of running which is different from that of an athlete. Since the player must be capable of sudden changes of direction or speed, it is important that the length of his stride, particularly when he is close to the ball, should not be as great as that of a sprinter or long distance runner. To facilitate sudden stops or quick changes of direction, the player should attempt to keep his centre of gravity relatively close to the ground.

To halt suddenly, the front leg is used as a brake and the other ceases to push off. The front leg is forced to bend because of the pressure against the ground and the force of the shifting centre of gravity is absorbed by a yielding, yet braced muscular system. The braking effect can be reinforced by leaning the upper part of the body backwards.

The player's centre of gravity must be kept low not only for a sudden stop but also when darting off into a gap. To move as fast and as energetically as possible, the joints should be kept slightly bent. This position is best suited for powerful acceleration and, therefore, for a quick movement into a gap.

The technique for changing direction is based essentially on the technique for making a sudden stop. As soon as the defender realises that the opposing player is going to stop or to change direction, he must reduce the length of his stride. This is necessary to ensure that the centre of gravity is kept as close to the ground as possible, which is, as has already been explained, a vital factor in being able to stop suddenly. The stop is then followed by the change of direction; this always starts with a firm bracing of the outside leg, that is to say, if the player changes direction left, the right leg is braced, while the left leg pushes out in the new direction. When this leg is braced, the rest of the body must be stationary with no movement towards the original direction.

After the push off the braced leg, all parts of the body strive to move in the new direction, assisted by stick and arms.

An important prerequisite for the fast, purposeful execution of a movement is a high degree of alertness, quite apart from the technical ability to be able to carry it out. A player with a low degree of alertness is unable to sum up the situation correctly in fractions of a second and to react in time. A hockey player's dexterity can be raised to the required level by following the programme set out below.

Preparatory exercises:

1. While running, touch the ground with one hand without stopping and run on.
2. Carry out a complete turn (anti-clockwise or clockwise) while running at top speed and continue straight ahead.

3. Carry out a half-turn (anti-clockwise and clockwise) while running at top speed and carry on running backwards (forwards).
4. Run alternately forwards, backwards and sideways.
5. Run sideways with a cross-over step. When the left (right) shoulder points in the direction along which the player is running, the right (left) leg is placed alternately in front of and then behind the left (right) leg.
6. Slalom between flags placed at varying distance along an arbitrarily curved line.
7. While running at top speed suddenly dodge off to the right or left.
8. Starting off from different positions (squatting, sitting, when lunging well forward, with legs wide apart, lying on the front, back, etc.) forwards, to the left, right and backwards.
9. On the coach's signal, the player breaks into a sprint from a walk.
10. While sprinting, the players come to a sudden halt when the whistle goes.

Exercises (see also p.137, '. . . games designed to gain experience in close marking').

1. Draw two additional lines between the goal-line and 22.90m line, as illustrated in *Fig. 135*. Four to five players stand on the goal-line. When the whistle goes, they run to the first line; the players stop there with one foot on it. From there they return to the goal-line which must be touched with the foot; they then run to the second line, after which they return to the first line, stepping on it and, finally, they run to the 22.90m line. The first runner to cross it is the most skilful and agile.

When stopping, the body should be slightly turned, in addition to

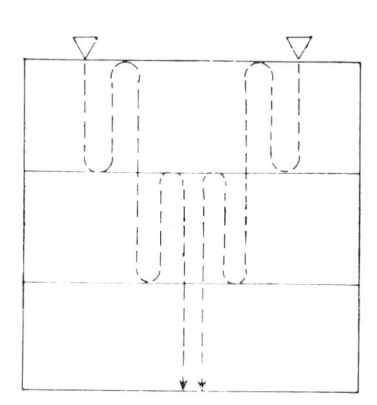

FIG. 135

keeping the centre of gravity as low as possible and the powerful bracing of the front leg to brake the forward movement.
2. The players stand on the goal-line. On the coach's whistle, they race towards the 22.90m line. Each time the whistle goes, the players wheel about immediately and run towards the line they are now facing. The first player to cross the line towards which he is running after the last whistle, is the winner.

   The coach should not whistle too frequently in the early runs. In this way, he will get the players to run fast and will prevent shirkers from winning. Later on he should whistle more frequently.
3. Two players run side by side 2m apart, starting slowly but then slightly speeding up later. A suddenly runs off at will, forwards, sideways or even backwards; B must follow each move, so as to preserve the same distance from his partner all the time.
4. A game of catch against the clock. The catcher must touch all the players, who keep within the circle, as quickly as possible. Players may each have a stick and ball, which they must dribble when catching.
5. Two players play catch around a goal.
6. The circle serves as a playing area for the eight to ten runners in it and two catchers compete against each other. Which one will be the first to make ten touches, without catching the same player twice running? Each touch is counted aloud. The players touched are neither eliminated nor do they take the place of their catcher. They continue to run around within the circle until one of the catchers has made ten touches.
7. The group of 8 players is divided into two equal sides. Each side is lined up within its own playing area, which is 10m square. A catcher from the opposing team enters each playing area; his task is to catch all the opposing runners as quickly as possible. When caught, players squat down and the remaining ones must run around them. The first catcher to touch all the opposing runners gains one point for his side. After two new catchers have been chosen, the game starts again.
8. Five players of one team go onto a marked out pitch (which is a 22.90m X 22.90m square), while the other team of five catchers lines up outside it. On the coach's whistle, the first catcher runs onto the pitch and catches a player from the opposing team as quickly as possible; he then leaves the pitch and touches the next catcher to send him on to the pitch. The coach notes the time taken by each team of catchers to make one catch each and the winning team is the one requiring the least time. The players touched on the pitch remain in play; they do not drop out.

   Variation: Each catcher has a particular opponent assigned to him, whom he has to catch.

9. Catching is made more difficult by allowing a player (holding his hands close to his body) to obstruct the catcher. If, in spite of this, the catcher manages to touch one of the ten runners within the circle, then the player obstructing takes the catcher's place, while the caught player obstructs.

All these games of catch serve to develop a player's dexterity, because they demand sudden changes of direction, variations in speed, skilful evasive movements and deceptive movements of the body — all of which should be mastered by every good player.

18 Some Very Short Notes about the Psychological Preparations

It occurs quite frequently that teams, as well as individual players, do not produce the performance in a match which would normally be expected of them, despite their great ability, both technically and tactically, and their excellent physical condition. Experience has also frequently shown that teams, or players, that are considered rather weak can play above themselves and are capable of producing outstanding performances. The reasons for this lie in the realm of psychology. The good coach knows that the team's, or the player's, ability does not depend merely on physical, technical and tactical qualities, but also on psychological considerations. Influencing these, so as to benefit performance, is one of the many important tasks that the coach has to master. If the coach is trying to prepare his players and his team psychologically to take part in a championship, he should consider the following points:

1. At the outset, the coach should take every care to see that a mutual trust exists among the players. Mutual good feelings and trust between players have frequently enough decided a game. The forwards can attack in a much more relaxed frame of mind when they can trust their halves and backs. The backs can, for their part, deal with attacks from the opposing forward line in a more relaxed way, if they know that they have a good goalkeeper behind them. A defender, whose play is not always faultless, will put up a radically better performance, if he knows that the player next to him is always ready to come to his assistance in a difficult situation. Through mutual assistance (not only during the match) arises a feeling of gratitude and team-spirit which is absolutely vital for the well-being of the team. The same feeling of gratitude is felt, for example, by the inside-left for the inside-right, when the latter unselfishly passes the ball to him for a shot at goal, instead of taking a shot himself from a rather more acute angle.

   Besides trusting each other, the players must also have a positive feeling of confidence in their own team. Only when this is shared by all the players will each individual's whole effort be exerted entirely for the benefit of his side rather than for his own personal advantage.
2. Furthermore, each player should have confidence not only in his side and his team-mates but also in himself. The player will only radiate self-confidence, sureness and activity, when he has no reservations, emotion-

ally, about the tasks appointed to him in the game and also when he recognises that he has received the best possible preparation for that game. He must be aware that he is up to the demands of the game. The knowledge that he has received the best possible preparation breeds a healthy self-confidence in every individual player. Theoretical preparation, too, can raise his self-confidence. It improves his sense of perspective, enables him to sum up situations more rapidly and to make quicker decisions.

A very important point, too, is the player's trust in his trainer. If this trust is missing, then coach and team should go their separate ways as soon as possible.

3. Apart from the proper organisation of the day's programme on the day of the big game, the most important single point in the psychological preparation of both the individual player and of the team is the drawing up of a tactical plan. The coach, and each individual player, tries to anticipate the difficulties and the obstacles which might confront the team during the match by imagining himself in the various situations that can arise in any championship game; further, he tries to form a clear idea of the opposition, and also of the conditions to be expected.

In drawing up his tactical plan, the coach should talk over the following three points with his players:

a) First of all, the opposition's plan of attack is analysed. Only when the opponents' likely tactics have been correctly analysed and preparations have been made to counter these tactics can the coach rest assured that a firm base of self-confidence and psychological adjustment has been created in all his players for the match.

b) After the analysis of the likely tactics to be adopted by the opponents, tactical instructions are given to individual players and to the team as a whole. Naturally, the coach will only specify such tasks as are appropriate to individual players' physical and mental capacities and to their technical and tactical capabilities. If, however, he does give a player a task which is beyond the latter's capabilities, the player may well go into the important game with a feeling of uncertainty which can, all too easily, be transmitted to his team-mates.

Whenever possible, the coach should discuss a specific tactical task with the player concerned and listen to his remarks and suggestions. This process of mutual discussion can have a positive effect on the player's attitude to the task allotted him, giving him the energy to see it through. Moreover, the coach can discover from the discussion whether the player has correctly understood his task.

c) Preparations are not yet over, however, when the tactical instructions

FIG. 136

have been given to individual players and to the whole team. Before the game, a good coach will draw the attention of his team to various contingencies and possible variations in their opponents' game, so that his players will be able to react to these quickly and actively in the match. As a result of this preparation, the element of surprise should be avoided, so that there is no reason for feelings of unsureness and nervousness. Rather, the player goes into the crucial game in an equable and confident frame of mind, since he now possesses a very clear idea of his opponents' likely actions, his own possible answers to these and the likely variations in his opponents' game.

Within the scope of this preparation, the coach must also clear up certain specific tactical queries, such as, for example, what to do when one's own side is leading shortly before the end of the game or when it is losing.

In addition, he will issue such tactical instructions as are necessary to cover special eventualities, for example, penalty corners, corners, free hits near the circle and penalty strokes.

At half time, the coach has a fresh opportunity to prepare his players psychologically for the second half.*

---

* see in '*The Advanced Science of Hockey*', the chapters 'Half-time Coaching' and 'Training without actual exercise'.

Quite calmly he should analyse, clearly and concisely, the opponents' methods and also comment in which aspects his own side has to improve in the second half. He should speak to each individual player in a different way, according to their psycho-physical qualities; he should try to adopt different methods to calm down unsteady players and emotional ones and he should speak to weaker players in a different fashion to those of greater talents. Apart from making constructive criticisms, he should praise good play where possible to raise the player's confidence still further. A certain amount of 'moral re-armament' is especially important when the side is losing and is beginning to give a pessimistic appearance.

In the course of this short survey of a player's general psychological preparation, the responsible role of the coach has surely been made plain. On his abilities as an instructor, and on his psychological insight, depends the extent to which he can apply psychology to the team's training and use it for the improvement of overall performance.